WHAT PEOP
ABOUT FLOR

In a small, concise paperback book, Ms. Gips has placed a tremendous amount of valuable information on the language of flowers while maintaining a very Victorian style with the use of numerous Victorian sketches and colored photos. The floral information is complete and accurate, and the dictionary of Flora's Sentiments is easy to use. This is a must-have book for those studying or enjoying the language of flowers.

James Moretz, Director,
American Floral Art School

I find that Kathleen Gips's book on the language of flowers is an excellent reference for programs for children and for all kinds of activities with plants. I use it to create meaningful flower arrangements and tussie-mussies. It contains great detail on the meaning of flowers and is well organized and thorough—I keep it right next to my desk so it's always there when I need it.

Holly H. Shimizu, Chief Horticulturist,
United States Botanic Garden

Flora's Dictionary is a delightful and accurate guide. I use it as my primary reference in the development of products based on herbal and floral meanings, when we design fresh tussie-mussies for weddings, and in class and lecture preparation.

Betsy Williams, Owner, The Proper Season

This delightful book, filled with flower lore, meanings, poetry, and old-fashioned wisdom, should be in every library. You will turn to it often when you give a tussie-mussie or a single bloom, or when you tuck a fragrant leaf into a special letter.

Betty H. Stevens, Past President,
The Herb Society of America

Flora's Dictionary is indispensable in our shop, where we're known for our herbs, wreaths, bouquets, and tussie-mussies for special occasions. Of the several books on this subject, we use *this one* as our florigraphic dictionary again and again. It's an important resource for our potpourri classes, part of our bride's display area, and in our garden books section. We can't keep it in stock around Valentine's Day and Mother's Day. It gives gardeners new design ideas for their home gardens, and it helps our customers give something extra special to their friends.

Lucia and Michael Bettler,
Owners, Lucia's Garden

This engaging little book can teach you a new language—one that's as much fun today as it was in Victorian England. Flowery sentiments will flow from your garden.

Kathleen Halloran, Editor,
The Herb Companion *magazine*

This beautiful, sentimental book on the meaning of flowers is a perfect gift for those who love herbs and flowers or are devotees of the Victorian era. I can envision a group of friends in the mid-1800s carefully selecting the appropriate flower for a tussie-mussie, wanting it to be the most meaningful possible.
This book is my choice for gifts for very special friends.

Jeri Schwartz, fine arts and antiques dealer and
member, International Society of Appraisers

If you want to "say it with flowers", this book will help you do just that. From Alyssum (worth beyond beauty) to Zinnia (thoughts of absent friends), this floral dictionary will help you say it best.

Debbie Cravens, Owner, Wood Violet Books

With 200 pages of floral dictionaries, plant symbolism, and quick reference guides, Kathleen Gips's *Flora's Dictionary* is a treat for tussie-mussie lovers, Anglophiles, and sentimental gift givers. Use it as a quick reference guide or read it cover to cover for a charming floral history lesson.

Herb Quarterly *magazine*

An indispensable guide for the tussie-mussie lover and those interested in the meanings of herbs and flowers.

Phyllis Shaudys, Author, The Pleasure of Herbs

Flora's Dictionary is about the most complete floral dictionary I have seen. It is a must for folklorists and students of horticultural history and Victoriana. If you are a floral designer or herbal wedding consultant, or offer classes or workshops, this book would be a real treat. I recommend it.

Paula Oliver, Editor,
The Business of Herbs *magazine*

FLORA'S

DICTIONARY

THE VICTORIAN LANGUAGE
OF HERBS AND FLOWERS

KATHLEEN GIPS

This book is dedicated, with pansies for thoughts and peppermint for warmth of feeling, to all Tussie-Mussie Ambassadors: herb ladies across the country who make and give herb and flower nosegays for every occasion. Their handmade posies speak the eloquent floral language with fragrance and beauty.

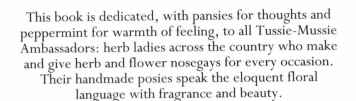

Copyright © 1990 Kathleen Gips

First edition published in 1987
Second edition (completely revised), June, 1990
Third edition (completely revised), September, 1995

Published by TM Publications
152 South Main Street, Chagrin Falls, Ohio 44022

Cover, text design, and editing by
David Merrill, Image Services

The hand-colored wreath on the cover of this book is reproduced from the title page of *Flora's Dictionary* by E.W. Wirt, published in 1829.

Printed in the United States by BookCrafters, Chelsea, Michigan 48118

ISBN 0-9648204-0-4   16.95

Library of Congress Catalog Number: 90-91662

Library of Congress
Cataloging-in-Publication Data:

GIPS, KATHLEEN
p. cm.
Includes index
ISBN 0-9648204-0-4
[1. Flower Language 2. Tussie
mussies 3. Plants—Folklore
4. Victoriana 5. Herbs—History
I. TITLE]
745.92'3 — dc20 90-91662
CiP

First Printing Sept. 1995
10 9 8 7 6 5 4 3 2 1

CONTENTS

ACKNOWLEDGMENTS

A special word of thanks to Nan Keenan for her gracious sharing and enthusiastic encouragement in my pursuit of fluency in florigraphy. Nan shares my intense interest in and insatiable curiosity about the language of plants.

I am also grateful to Mr. James Moretz, curator and director of the American Floral Art School in Chicago, Illinois, who has very generously provided information on the Victorian uses of flowers, the floral language, and the tussie-mussie from his worldwide resources.

Keith Crotz, *The American Botanist,* and Elizabeth Woodburn Books have been very helpful in locating the antiquarian floral dictionaries used in my continuing research.

Great appreciation is extended to David Merrill as an editor and creative designer in helping to make my ideas a reality.

Finally, but most importantly, unending thanks and love go to my husband, Jack, a constant support and an invaluable proofreader.

FOREWORD

Among my many treasured collections, I especially cherish my small pile of old floral dictionaries. It's small only because they are themselves such little books. In this case, however, size bears no relationship to content: they are enchanting volumes, filled with collected wisdom and whimsey.

Through the millenia, people have used plants for food, housing, medicine, and pleasure. Fragrance and beauty were obvious attributes that everyone admired and enjoyed, and they were utilized in ever widening ways. Religious rites were made more powerful by the addition of plants, and magic also was influenced by them.

Eventually, the awesome wonders of plant lore outgrew the obvious. People began to imbue them with deeper, hidden meanings, symbolism and messages developed from endless usage and years of close observation. The little books in my collection speak of these quiet virtues.

Today's frenzied lifestyle makes one marvel at the patience required to determine which plants best conveyed "love" (rose), "the return of happiness" (lily of the valley), "luck" (lavender), or "domestic tranquility" (sage). My favorite is "energy in adversity", the meaning attributed to the lowly chamomile, which thrives under adverse conditions, is used as a tea, a dye plant, an astringent, a sedative, and a fungicide, and is also eminently charming. All that takes energy!

It has always been my greatest delight to delve into my collection to select flowers with just the right message for a dear friend, for someone who is grieving, or to celebrate an anniversary. A posy bearing such quaint eloquence sometimes proves to be the best of all gifts.

Now Kathleen Gips has put all this knowledge, the accumulated wisdom of centuries, into one incredibly concise and practical volume, the one I reach for whenever an occasion is well served by a floral message. Although I still value the little gems I've collected over the years, this book is the most useful of them all to "speak through herbs and flowers." Thank you, Kathleen, for compiling it for us.

To say it with herbs and flowers, I send you a sweet posy of coreopsis for "cheerful smiles", pansies for "good thoughts", bay with yarrow for "lasting success", and sage "to keep you healthy." Oh, yes, and lots of rosemary—"that's for remembrance."

Bertha Reppert, The Rosemary House
Mechanicsburg, Pennsylvania
May Day, 1995

A FLORAL OFFERING

*By all those token flowers, that tell
What words can never speak so well.*

—Byron

Herbs and flowers have been used throughout the ages to convey messages of beauty and love, offered at happy celebrations and occasions of sadness as symbols of love and friendship, encouragement and hope. This language of flowers is used today as it has been throughout the centuries. Flowers serve as messengers when words will not suffice or cannot be spoken.

The Victorians, enamored of flowers and messages of love, raised the floral language to its highest level. Each plant was assigned its own meaning. Victorians delighted in expressing thoughts and "speaking" to each other with combinations of plants. Ladies and gentlemen, young and old, studied dictionaries of plant meanings and practiced their teachings. Gardens of flowers and herbs were cultivated to create "word posies" or nosegays with a message.

In the past few decades, a growing fascination with herbs has increased interest in floral communication. Tussie-mussies—herb and flower nosegays—are part of every herb lady's repertoire, and countless gardeners carefully tend age-old herbs and old-fashioned flowers.

My interest in tussie-mussies and my intense pursuit of information about the language of herbs and flowers coincides with the current interest in Victoriana and an increasing demand for lectures on the subject. Those teaching opportunities have introduced me to many enthusiastic learners—new and experienced gardeners who are eager to share their bounty by creating symbolic nosegays for special recipients and occasions. The beauty, fragrance, and customized meanings of these handmade gifts are welcome personal messages in today's fast-paced world.

This second edition is my floral offering, presenting the language of herbs and flowers as fully as possible to those who have had difficulty finding sources of this information. Response to the first edition has been exciting and rewarding. Stories have come from people around the country who have used *Flora's Dictionary* in creating floral gifts with special sentiments: making tussie-mussies for a hospice or to placate a policeman who's just written a traffic ticket; creating potpourri, wreaths, and pressed-flower pictures with symbolic meanings; writing an herbal poem using florigraphy; planting a peace garden of herbs in a sculpture park or a floral language garden at the U.S. Botanic Garden; and planning an herbal curriculum for school children in New York City. A friend in Virginia won a blue ribbon at a flower show using the language of flowers as her category.

Symbolic meanings of plants, as expressed in this book, are gleaned from many old floral dictionaries discovered in antique bookstores. I have scoured floral dictionaries written between 1829 and 1869 to document the Victorian practice of communicating with botanical symbols. This information on plant meanings, and the poems and illustrations that embellish them, have been drawn directly from those sources. Most plants have more than one meaning, and all of these meanings have been incorporated here.

Some plants that are popular today were not grown in Victorian gardens. I created meanings for a few of these plants in the manner of the Victorians. For example, feverfew was absent in most of the old references. The origin of the word "feverfew" is "pyrethrum", which means "fire" and refers to the hot taste of the plant's root. I assigned the meaning "You light up my life" to this plant. The old floral dictionaries explain the origins of plant meanings, and I have included many of these explanations for the reader's pleasure.

Many of the Victorian plant favorites have waned in popularity or have been hybridized into extinction. Some plant names included in this dictionary may not be familiar today. However, gardeners and nursery owners are becoming increasingly interested in these old varieties and are seeking to increase their availability.

Flora's Dictionary is the second revised edition of *The Language of Flowers*. It represents the inevitable result of continuous research and includes information from additional earlier references and expansions of many meanings. This book will further the reader's knowledge of florigraphy, the Victorian language of flowers.

To quote Mrs. Wirt in her floral dictionary of 1829:

> There are few little presents more pleasing to a Lady than a bouquet of flowers; and if the donor be disposed to give them greater significance, it will be easy, with the manual before them, to make his selection in such a way as to stamp intelligence and simple expression on a simple posy.

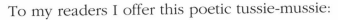

To my readers I offer this poetic tussie-mussie:

A bit of rosemary for your presence revives me,
with a rose for beauty and love,

circled with
>   *pinks, bonds of affection*
>   *honeysuckle, ties that bind*

adding a few stems of
>   *lemon verbena, enchantment*
>   *burnet, joy*
>   *tarragon, unselfish sharing, and*
>   *sage, esteem*

gathered together and surrounded by
>   *rose-scented geranium leaves, preference, and*
>   *fern fronds, fascination.*

Kathleen Gips
Chagrin Falls, Ohio

FLORA'S LANGUAGE

Mignonette
"Your qualities surpass your charms"

Heliotrope
"I love you"

Red carnation
"Pure and ardent love"

**"Your qualities surpass your charms.
I love you with a pure and ardent love."**

I sent my love clematis. She, walking white
  In her garden, reading Rossetti, veiled her sight
Under blue eyelids, blushingly comprehended
  *Her **mental beauty** was thereby commended.*

My love sent me the bud of a white rose
  *To say **her heart knew naught of love.** Repose*
*Fled from my days, to tell her of my **flame***
  I sent an iris. Swift her answer came;

She had gathered mouse-eared chickweed, flowers which swear
  ***Ingenuous simplicity**. Despair*
*Seized me, I sent gum cistus, saying: **"Tomorrow***
  ***I die."** She sent me yew, expressing **sorrow**.*

True to my word, I died; and to my tomb
  She mourning came. Her hat was all abloom
*With rosemary, which vows **not to forget**,*
  *And rue, to tell the world of her **regret**.*

But when upon my grave, my life, my dove,
  *Stooped to plant myrtle, signifying **love**,*
Then garden daisies in my dust were bred,
  *And "Sweet, **I share your***
  ***sentiments**," they said.*

  —Randolph Stow

LETTER FROM A VICTORIAN MAIDEN

June 15, 1836

My dear Anne,

Imagine my delight when upon the occasion of the afternoon of my nineteeth birthday, a bouquet was delivered from the object of my enamoured affections. The composition was elegant and beautiful, but the message sent a blush to my cheeks. He sent a red carnation, meaning pure and ardent love, blue violets for affection, pansies for thoughts, sweet William for a smile, iris for message, and hawthorn for hope. All these were surrounded by fern for sincerity and sweet geranium leaves for preference. Who could be more fortunate than I?

The gift of an already well used dictionary from my brother last Christmas has proved invaluable to identify the flowers contained in this message and to correctly decode the appropriate meanings. The sentiments of meanings allowed me to form a botanical response to his professed interest.

Constraint will be appropriate for fear of showing return of my true affections too soon. At the dinner party tonight I shall carry a dainty nosegay with the answer to his floral message. I will gather daisies for I will think of it, sweet marjoram for blushes (sent with appropriate modest decorum), goldenrod for indecision, with a few cornflowers (hope) and sprigs of lavender (faithfulness) tucked in for fear he may become discouraged without a sign of encouragement from me.

Sent with endearing affection to my closest friend,

Cecelia

A gift of flowers universally symbolizes love and caring thoughts. Conveying specific messages through the giving of herbs, flowers, and plants is known as the language of flowers.

Speaking in this enchanting, silent way flourished in the early nineteenth century. People expressed flowery thoughts by exchanging bouquets composed of carefully chosen plant words. Such communication usually revolved around feelings of love. Some plants conveyed a simple one-word meaning, such as loyalty (lavender) or sincerity (fern). Others might signify flirtatious sentences with messages of acceptance (feverfew, "I reciprocate your affection") or rejection (dandelion, "I find your presumptions laughable"). The definitions of these flower meanings, which were printed in dozens of floral dictionaries, are collectively called florigraphy.

THE AGE OF FLOWERS

This romantic and secretive form of communication became popular at the beginning of the nineteenth century. "Speaking" or communicating with flowers instead of words was the logical outcome of the Victorian passion for gardening, flowers, and plants. Nature and the study of botany were important concerns of the day. The pursuit and cultivation of plants and

Flora, The Goddess of Flowers

flowers occupied much of the leisure time of wealthy ladies, who were expected to be knowledgeable in all areas of botany and plant life.

> Happy the young and light hearted maiden, who, ignorant of the silly pleasures of the world, feels no occupation to be more agreeable than the study of plants. . . . Every morning a fresh harvest of flowers repays her diligent cultivation; a garden is to her an inexhaustible source of delight and instruction. By a charming art these beautiful productions of nature are converted into liquid perfumes, precious essences, or valuable conserves.
>
> Anonymous, *The Sentiment of Flowers,* 1840

The romantic movement immediately preceding the Victorian era placed great emphasis on poetry and pictures which incorporated flowers and their symbolism. During this rather proper age, it was more suitable for a young lady to adorn herself with flowers than with jewelry. With the reign of Queen Victoria, flowers gained a regal status. They were thought to have been created by God as the voices of Nature, capable of expressing feelings of friendship and love in a language that uses no written words. These "natural voices" had been purposely scattered over the earth.

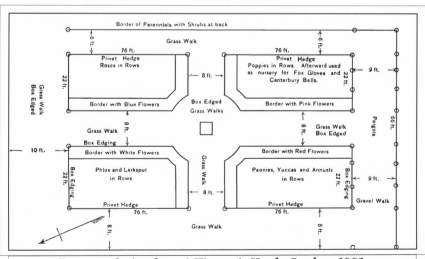

Parterre design from* A Woman's Hardy Garden, *1903.

> The interpreters of our sweetest sentiments, flowers lend their charms even to love. . . . The expression of this divine passion ought to be divine also, and it was to illustrate this that flowers were ingeniously made emblematical of our most delicate sentiments; they do, in fact, utter in "silent eloquence" a language better than writing; they are the delicate symbols of the illusions of a tender heart and of a lively and brilliant imagination.
>
> *The Sentiment of Flowers, 1840*

Nature, plants, and flowers were the rage of the day. Influenced by Queen Victoria (1839-1901), who loved flowers, the public became obsessed with growing flowers in the garden, wearing them on apparel, and using them in cosmetics and perfumes, as home decorations, and as the subjects of paintings and poems as well as in cooking. The emphasis on floriculture centered on meticulous gardening of the parterre—ornamental gardens with paths between the beds—which the Victorians created throughout their landscapes.

> Flower gardening is preeminently a woman's occupation and diversion. Nearly every great lady in England takes a personal interest in her gardens and conservatories, and knows all about the plants and flowers.
>
> Helena Rutherfurd Ely,
> *A Woman's Hardy Garden*, 1903

During this plant obsession, the Victorians began attributing lifelike qualities to flowers. Flowers gained the power to extract one's feelings and to interpret these feelings from thoughts into words.

Life Among the Flowers

Musings on Flowers
Flowers, of all created things the most innocently simple, and most superbly complex; playthings for

childhood, ornaments of the grave, and companions of the cold corpse!— flowers, beloved by the wandering idiot, and studied by the deep thinking man of science!—flowers, that, of perishing things, are the most heavenly!—flowers, that unceasingly expand to heaven their grateful, and to man their cheerful, looks; partners of human joy; soothers of human sorrow; fit emblems of the victor's triumphs, of the young bride's blushes; welcome to the crowded halls, and graceful upon solitary graves!—flowers are in the volume of nature what the expression "God is love" is in the volume of the revelation. What a desolate place would be a world without a flower! It would be a face without a smile—a feast without a welcome. Are not flowers the stars of the earth, and are not our stars the flowers of heaven? One cannot look closely at the structure of a flower without loving it. They are emblems and manifestations of God's love to the creation, and they are the means and ministrations of man's love to his fellow-creatures.

Greenwood, *Rural Wreath:*
Life Among the Flowers, 1855

Roses were of particular importance. Each variety of rose was ascribed a meaning. Many pages were devoted to roses in the old floral dictionaries. As the "Queen of the Flowers", it inspired many rosy phrases: rosy complexion, everything's rosy, lovely as a rose. Roses, flowers, and nature were desired as a part of life. Gardens were thought to be rooms or extensions of the home. Flowers were enthusiastically grown and used in every Victorian home.

Henrietta Dumont, in her 1868 book, *The Floral Offering,* tells her readers the reasons for flowers and explains the importance of being able to interpret nature correctly.

Roses were of
particular importance.

Why do flowers enter and shed their perfume over every scene of life, from the cradle to the grave?. . . It is for no other reason than that flowers have in themselves a real and natural significance. They have a positive relation to man, his sentiments, passions, and feelings. They correspond to actual emotions. They have their mission—a mission of love and mercy. They have their language, and from the remotest ages this language has found its interpreters.

Recent writers in all languages recognise the beauty and propriety of this language to such an extent, that an acquaintance with it has now become indispensable as a part of a polished education.

A PROPER FLORAL EDUCATION

The floral language was intricate and involved—characteristics typical of the Victorian lifestyle. Dictionary authors encouraged floral silent communication. Their Victorian readers valued gentility and modesty. They read with delight the suggestions of mingling ordinary gardening chores and romance. Authors recommended

Bringing in the flowers

that a walk through the garden could carry on a conversation of admiration, humor, and pleasantry. This seemed a welcome amusement for Victorian lady gardeners with time to devote to gentle pursuits.

With fan and flowers

Most floral sentiments were related to feelings or affairs of the heart, and especially to love and emotions associated with loving feelings: they were not useful in asking the time of day or recording a cake recipe. The floral language provided a means for those who were unable to speak or pen a romantic poem to express their inclinations for love by gathering appropriate flowers. Verbal expression of ardor was discouraged in proper Victorian culture, and the silent floral language became an acceptable and often preferred way to share sentiments such as love, hate, jealousy, friendship, gratitude, happiness, and grief.

> No spoken word can approach to the delicacy of sentiment
> to be inferred from the timously offered flower, and the
> softest impressions may be thus conveyed without offence,
> and even a profound grief alleviated, at a moment when the
> most tuneful voice would grate harshly on the ear, and the
> stricken soul can be soothed only by an act of grateful silence.
> Anonymous, *The Language of Flowers,* 1835

Both ladies and gentlemen were expected to be well versed in floral communication, as noted in the dedication of Sarah Hale's 1832 book, *Flora's Interpreter:*

Because flowers had to be correctly named before one
could discern their messages, learning botany and plant
identification was an important part of each young lady's
education. This scientific aspect gave validity and a sense
of purpose to naming flowers and translating their
messages.

However, the elaborate, detailed, and complicated floral
language could only be mastered by those who spent their
lives learning it. Young ladies of the era cultivated these
talents at finishing schools that offered courses in floral
communication as well as art, music, and needlework.
This learning was an indispensable part of the polished
education of all proper ladies. Floral dictionaries were the
source of this information.

> The language of flowers has recently attracted so much
> attention that an acquaintance with it seems to be deemed, if
> not an essential part of polite education, at least a graceful
> and elegant accomplishment. A volume furnishing a complete
> interpretation of those meanings most generally attached to
> flowers, has therefore become a desirable if not an essential
> part of a gentleman's or a lady's library.
> Catherine Waterman, *Flora's Lexicon,* 1839

The proliferation of floral dictionaries during the
nineteenth century seems to indicate that floral
communication was a part of everyday life. Actually,
though, little is mentioned about it in the popular
publications of the day, and some authors have
questioned whether florigraphy served as an actual form
of communication or simply as a pleasant diversion for
ladies with an abundance of free time. The *Ladies' Home
Journal* from 1885 to 1889 contains no mention of floral
communication, although it includes regular feature
articles about flowers for decorating homes, yards, and
dress. Flowers were an important part of the lifestyle, but

how much silent floral communication actually took place is uncertain. It was likely a pursuit only of the fashionable elite, even though the meanings of flowers, herbs, and other plants were commonly known.

In the preface to her 1829 *Flora's Dictionary* (the first American floral dictionary), Mrs. E.W. Wirt gives the reason for printing her version of floral meanings:

> The Lady who has given her leisure hours to this little play of fancy, has not the vanity to attach any serious consequence to it. The bagatelle, she trusts, is too light to attract the grave censure of the critic by profession. It has been an innocent recreation to herself; and it is with no higher expectation than of affording the like amusement to others, that it is now given to the press.

Mrs. Wirt candidly admits that her illustrated floral vocabulary book was created for her own enjoyment, and that it was finally printed because she had tired of penning many copies for friends.

In 1853, editor Laura Greenwood suggested that her dictionary, *The Rural Wreath,* was written ". . . to diversify the monotony of a long winter evening, to beguile the languid hours of a summer day, or to cheer the tedious convalescence of illness—its counsels and companionship will be found most soothing and sweet."

Most dictionaries differed slightly in their choices of meanings. Occasionally, a plant meaning would remain constant through decades of authors. Narcissus always meant egotism, for example. Most often, though, there was a plethora of meanings for the reader to choose. The recipient of a bouquet must have trembled at the notion of choosing an incorrect missive. Considering the hopelessness of correct communication, perhaps this supports the view that a floral dictionary was like a garden—a thing of pleasure and an enjoyable amusement.

FOUNDATIONS OF FLOWER LORE

Today, flowers speak in a simple, general language that is recognized by many, but the specialized form of communication that was popularized in the Victorian Era has ancient roots. The meanings of plants, in one form or another, were universally recognized and practiced in Europe for centuries. A century ago, the origins of many floral meanings were attributed to the Egyptians, Greeks, and Romans.

> The hieroglyphics of the ancient Egyptians abound in floral symbols, and from this we may surmise that the Greeks became accustomed to this figurative language. Their poetical fables are full of the metamorphoses of their deities into plants; indeed, there was no flower to which their imaginations had not affixed some meaning.
> *The Sentiment of Flowers,* 1840

THE DOCTRINE OF SIGNATURES

According to a popular European theory called the Doctrine of Signatures, plants were thought to be marked by God to designate their medicinal uses, and each plant was used in treating the disease or part of the anatomy that its botanical characteristics indicated or resembled. These relationships between the characteristics of plants and their roles in healing were the bases of many plant meanings. The walnut was thought to resemble the brain and was used in treating diseases of the brain; and the meaning assigned to walnut was "intellect". The generic Latin name for sage is *Salvia,* which means "to save", because sage was thought to be a universal cure for many diseases; and the meaning assigned to sage was "long life and good health". Because the shape of the heartsease flower resembles that of a human heart, a syrup made from the flowers was used in treating diseases of the heart; and the meaning assigned to this flower was "happiness", which was thought to originate in the heart.

Pensées.
ATTACHEMENT
Le mien s'accroît chaque jour.

Authors garnered plant symbolisms from every possible source. In addition to plagiarizing prior dictionaries, they quoted meanings referenced in the Bible and classic literature. Shakespeare, whose extensive knowledge of plant symbolism showed in his writings, was frequently quoted in floral dictionaries in support of a given sentiment. The phrase from Hamlet—"There's rosemary, that's for remembrance"—referred to the popular belief that rosemary restored the memory.

> In Europe, the language of flowers has existed and been recognised for long ages among the people, although scarcely noticed by the literati until a comparatively recent period. Shakespeare, however, who nothing escaped which was known to the people, exhibits his intimate acquaintance with the language of flowers in his masterly delineation of the madness of Ophelia.
>
> Henrietta Dumont, *The Floral Offering,* 1868

In addition to Egyptian hieroglyphics, Greek and Roman mythology, the Bible, religious beliefs, natural plant appearance, and medieval medicinal use, plant meanings were derived from legends, folk tales, myths, and classical poetry and literature. Flower color and fragrance also were thought to affect meaning. For example, the color white symbolized purity and youth: thus, the white violet indicated "modesty and innocence", whereas the blue violet meant "faithfulness and sweetness".

THE SECRETIVE SELAM

One other significant source of plant meanings in the Victorian language of flowers was the Selam language, a rhyming Turkish language based on objects rather than words—a type of written code whose communication was unspoken and which was used in harems for secret communication. Many of the old floral dictionaries make reference to the East and the Selam language.

Love hath its symbols; hence in Cathay,
  And where the arrowy Tigris rolls his wave,
The fragrant reeds and woods, whose bending trunks
  Weep precious balms; and on whose palmy fields

Where erst the majesty of Persia fell,
  The words of passion find an utterance thus,
And all its nameless feelings stand revealed
  By emblems gathered from grove and rill.

Methinks our land, as fair and green as these,
  Might furnish matter, in its mossy glades
And fern-invested rills, where thought should rove
  And young imagination sport as free.
          J. F. Hollings in *The Flower Vase,*
                  Miss S. C. Edgarton, 1847

In the late 1700s in England and Europe, people generally looked upon flowers as unnecessary, but in the Far East, flowers were thought of as the "alphabet of the angels." They were used, along with fruits, silks, and pictures, as a substitute for words to express feelings.

The Sentiment of Flowers in 1840 credited Lady Mary Whortley Montagu, the wife of an English ambassador to Turkey, as one of the first to mention the language of flowers in England. According to the *Encyclopedia Britannica,* she was "the most colorful Englishwoman of her time." The tale goes that Lady Mary became so enamored with this secret communication of love that she wrote many letters describing it to her friends in England in the year 1718.

> Her ladyship states that there is no flower without a verse belonging to it, and that it is possible to quarrel, reproach, or send a letter of passion, friendship, or civility, or even of news, without ever inking the fingers.

The exact messages were expressed with tokens and objects rather than words. Her letters and references to them are quoted in many floral dictionaries.

> Lady M. W. Montagu was one of the first to introduce floral language to Europe. When at Pera, she sent a Turkish

love letter to a friend in England, from which we extract the botanical emblems.

Clove: You are as slender as this clove!
         You are an unblown rose!
         I have long loved you, and you have not known it.

Jonquil: Have pity on my passion!

A rose: May you be pleased,
         and your sorrows mine!

***Illustration from* The Poetry
of Flowers, A Book for All Seasons**

| *A straw:* | Suffer me to be your slave! |
| *Pepper:* | Send me an answer. |

The Sentiment of Flowers, 1840

Her letters were published in 1763 after her death. Due to the concurrent interest in flowers and botany, they were eagerly accepted in England.

Although many of the floral dictionaries make reference to it, there is some question whether this Eastern language actually was a basis for Victorian flower meanings. Comparison between the above reference and plant

meanings listed in nineteenth-century floral dictionaries yields no apparent connection between the two "languages". Several other dictionaries also claim to use Lady Montagu's letters as a basis for their floral definitions, but this connection is difficult to prove. Clove, pear, straw, cinnamon, and pepper are not listed at all in any of those dictionaries, and the common European meanings given for the jonquil ("desire") and the rose ("beauty") do not support the Turkish botanical emblems. Reference to the meanings from the East is, in fact, made only in the introduction. Perhaps, as Mrs. Wirt suggests, few of the Eastern emblems ever actually reached the pages of the floral dictionaries.

> It is upon the hint suggested by this Oriental custom, and for the purpose of trying, as a matter of curiosity, how far this emblematic language could be carried, that the following collection has been made. Mr. Percival tells us,
>
> *"Each blossom that blooms in their garden bowers*
> *On its leaves a mystic language bears."*
>
> Pity it is that we have no key to this mystic language of the East. Very few of their emblems have reached us.
>
> *Flora's Dictionary,* 1829

One possible explanation for the lack of Selam meanings in European floral dictionaries is the then-current royalty's passion for flowers, which might well have caused many of the symbolic objects of the East to be substituted with the more popular and accessible European flowers.

VICTORIAN FLORAL DICTIONARIES

FLOWER MANUAL FRENZY

Nineteenth-century interest in botany resulted in an abundance of dictionaries explaining plant symbolism. Ladies demanded information on all aspects of botany, including the popular language of the flora. Before the appearance of specific floral dictionaries, herbal and floral significance was explained in botanical texts and practical books on gardening. As the demand for information increased and printing capabilities improved, dozens of floral dictionaries began to be marketed in France, England, and America.

Many books on floral meanings were available between the years 1820 and 1890. They were attractive books with engraved leather bindings and gilt-edged pages. Some were small, made to be carried easily in hand, so a young lady or gentleman would always be prepared to translate an unexpected floral message. Illustrations were limited, printed from hand-engraved plates, and the delicate printed drawings of floral bouquets were individually painted with beautiful watercolors. Many of the volumes included blank pages between which flowers or leaves could be pressed for future communications.

Floral dictionaries became gifts for graduation from finishing school and for birthdays and holidays. There is clear evidence that floral dictionaries were well read by their owners. Many still contain remnants and brown imprints of pressed flowers and leaves within their pages. Newspaper clippings about flowers or containing floral poems are tucked into many copies, and pencilled notations of names and dates appear under the poems. Most floral dictionaries were published in numerous revised editions, which attests to their popularity. Sarah Hale's *Flora's Interpreter* is said to have had seventeen.

The floral dictionaries of the 1800s listed flowers, herbs, vines, shrubs, trees, and even weeds which grew in windowboxes, greenhouses, gardens, fields, and forests. Even a walk through the woods could speak: mushroom

Hand-colored engraved plate from Flora's Interpreter, *1833.*

for suspicion, moss for maternal affection, oak for strength, fern for fascination. The plants were listed alphabetically in dictionary format, though occasionally an author listed the plants by their meanings or by the seasons of the year.

For each plant, most authors included a poem, usually classical, along with the meaning and botanical description. After this poem, which mentioned the plant, came a "sentiment", a poem that expressed the plant's meaning. A poetic "answer" to the sentiment poem was often included for the occasion when a floral answer was desired.

The more complete editions of floral dictionaries contained botanical explanations, including growing characteristics and special growing habits, native habitats,

Original pressed leaves from the author's copy of
Flora's Interpreter (1833). The handwritten inscription reads,
"June 2, 1858: Friendship is love without wings."

cultivation techniques, and common uses. This information can be useful in determining which plant was being referred to. Latin botanical names were listed in the dictionaries only occasionally. Where they did appear, they were the names given by Linneaus, which often differed from today's names for the same plants because plant family division and nomenclature have been revised.

The same plant often was called different names by different authors, depending on locality and colloquial names. For example, *Campanula* was listed variously as bachelor button, blue bottle, cornflower, and centura. These variations, coupled with the often obsolete Latin botanical names, can lead to confusion in determining the specific plant to which the authors of the 1800s were referring. To compound this problem, many vintage plants have vanished. What plant is known today as the "squirting cucumber" or the "moving plant"?

Unusual plants such as the Venus fly trap (deceit) or the night-blooming cereus (transient beauty) were of great interest. A large variety of unusual plants from around the world were collected and coveted by the Victorians, and many unfamiliar plants appear in most dictionaries. Cowslip ("You are my angel") and ice plant ("Your looks freeze me") are rarely grown in today's gardens.

Madame Charlotte de la Tour (a pseudonym: her real name was Louise Cortambert) compiled the earliest documented floral dictionary, a celebrated French publication called *Le Langage des Fleurs*. First printed in Paris in 1818 and subsequently reprinted in 18 editions, it was translated into many languages. It was the basis of dozens of dictionaries that followed, including pirated versions in Spain and America.

> Some years ago the Editor of this little volume met with that popular and celebrated French publication, 'Le Langage des Fleurs,' by Madame de la Tour. Struck with the ingenuity of its construction, he translated a part. . . . He now ventures to offer the result of his labours to the world.
>
> *The Sentiment of Flowers,* 1840

Madame de la Tour derived plant meanings from

ancient Greek and Roman traditions, ancient and current literature, and folklore as well as the uses and botanical characteristics of the plants. Parts of her collection of meanings were thought to be based on the Selam language.

Sarah Hale—herself a prolific writer—was determined to use popular American authors as the source of poetry for

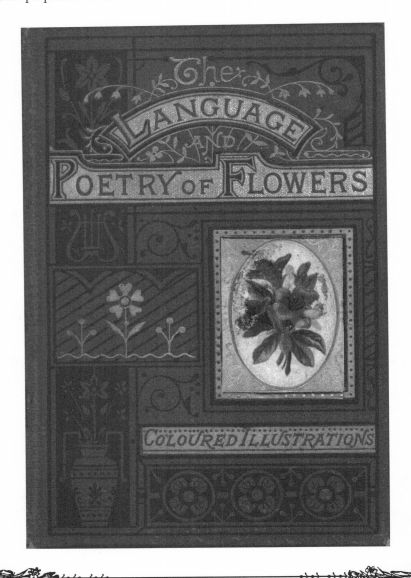

her edition. She expressed pride in her 1833 book, *Flora's Interpreter,* because she did so rather than using the more common English verse.

> In arranging this little work, it was my purpose to combine, with the names and remembrances of flowers, a selection of sentiments from our best poets. I hoped my experiment would give an increased interest to botanical researches among young people, at least; and among all classes would promote a better acquaintance with the beauties of our own literature. There is nothing new attempted, except in the arrangement, and introduction of American sentiments.

In the early *printed* floral dictionaries, most sentiments and their origins were drawn from the first *written* floral dictionary: authors varied the wordings slightly, perhaps to avoid direct plagiarism. It is no surprise, then, that similar meanings occur quite often in the earlier works.

Stock

> Though the system of Madame de la Tour has been adopted, it must be understood that this work is not a mere translation. Great care has been taken to add such information as was required to render the work complete, and a discretion has been exercised in the rejection or alteration of those passages not suited to the English taste.

The Stock has been made the emblem of lasting beauty; because, though it is less graceful than the rose and less majestic than the lily, its splendour is more durable and its fragrance of longer continuance.

The Floral Offering, 1868

To use the floral language in the nineteenth century amidst this proliferation of dictionaries, it must have been essential that the sender and receiver of a flower message use the ***same*** dictionary in order to interpret correctly the silent communication!

The selection of different plants with similar meanings was usually vast, which allowed the composer of floral messages to choose from among the flowers that were blooming at any time throughout the season.

ASSIGNING BOTANICAL MEANINGS

Each dictionary author edited and interpreted the meaning of each plant and gave the associated source. Throughout the century, the meanings assigned to a given plant in the different dictionaries were variations of the same sentiments, and plagiarism was common. With more than 150 floral dictionaries in print, no two authors were in complete agreement. For example, in the first part of the century, the white poppy was listed as meaning "consolation of sleep", and in the second half of the century by a different author as "sleep of the heart". Both refer to the effect of the opiate within the poppy seeds, though each uses different words. Such differences can be very confusing for the serious student of the language of flora.

Authors often assigned different meanings to the same plant. In her 1839 book, *Flora's Lexicon,* Catherine Waterman refers to balm (*Melissa officinalis*) as meaning "sympathy"; yet Tyas, in his 1869 book, *The Language of Flowers* (a popular and often-used title), assigned the meaning "pleasantry" to the same plant. The books were written decades apart, and the information given about the plant is the same, yet the authors derived different meanings for it. Clearly, meanings were assigned or revised according to the authors' own insights and personal interpretations, and documenting the exact meanings as the Victorians intended them can be quite a challenge.

However, many meanings also varied—sometimes significantly—by locality and according to the author's interpretation. Toward the late nineteenth century, modest authors altered many earlier meanings to make them less suggestive and therefore more in keeping with proper Victorian culture. For example, the hollyhock's ability to freely reseed itself earned it the meaning "fruitful in offspring" in the early half of the century, but this was later changed to the more symbolic and proper "foresight". Laura Greenwood, author of the 1853 dictionary, *Life Among the Flowers,* assures readers that the presentation of her work is "unexceptional in taste and morals."

If previous sources did not indicate a meaning for a flower that was commonly grown in the home and garden, Victorian authors felt free to select plant characteristics from which to create a sentiment, and to add it to their lists of meanings.

Mrs. Wirt admits, in her 1829 *Flora's Dictionary,* that a large portion of the meanings included in her work were created by her to supplement those she had gleaned from ancient and Eastern sources. This was justifiable because, by giving meanings to the popular plants of the day, Mrs. Wirt increased the floral communicative abilities of her readers.

> A few, and but a few of them have been arbitrarily assumed, and this only from the necessity of giving sufficient range and variety to this symbolic language.
> *Flora's Dictionary,* 1829

With such creativity added to diligent research, the number of published plant meanings had mounted into the hundreds by the end of the nineteenth century. Authors felt that plant meanings would be obvious to the reader if they merely discerned plant characteristics. This is often true: for example, morning glory with its climbing tendrils means "ties that bind". But how many readers would guess that ivy geranium means "May I have your hand for the next quadrille?"

Considering the intricate implications of what are, to us moderns, minor plant characteristics (such as location and the direction of presentation), it is easy to understand why so many dictionaries were written to explain this floral language. Deciphering exact meanings probably presented even the Victorians with an occasional challenge.

FLUENT FLORIGRAPHY

T he Victorian culture placed great emphasis on flower cultivation and use. Flowers were given human characteristics, so it seemed logical that they could also speak, using their own language. This language required as much study as French or Latin, and the Victorian ladies pursued it with vigor. This floral vernacular required documentation with dictionaries for reference. Speaking with flowers was termed "florigraphy".

Meanings were ascribed to a vast array of botanicals. Vegetables such as lettuce (cold-hearted) and pumpkin (bulkiness) were included, along with grains (wheat for prosperity) and spices (cinnamon for wisdom).

flo-rig′ra-phy (flō-rig′-ra-fē), n. [L. *flos, floris,* flower + –graphy.] The language or symbolism of flowers, as expressed in historical literature.
Webster's New International Dictionary of the English Language, 1955

In addition to the individual meanings for each flower and plant, emblems were often formed by grouping flowers with related meanings. Bouquets expressed more complex sentiments and were popular as illustrations in the floral dictionaries of the 1800s.

For example, a gentleman whose love was refused by the lady of his choice might present her with a bouquet of forget-me-nots (true love or forget me not), hawthorn (hope), and lily of the valley (return of happiness). This floral bouquet would say to his loved one, "Forget me not! In that rests my hope for the return of happiness." A floral response to discourage his affections might have been the lowly dandelion, meaning "Your presumptions are laughable!" or, to encourage his affections, the pretty pansy for "You occupy my thoughts."

THE INTRICACIES OF FLORAL SPEECH

There were special instructions for the placement of the flowers as they were presented; the meaning of a flower could be altered simply by a change in the direction in which it was given. A flower inclined to the right implied the first person, whereas one inclined to the left indicated the second person. For example, a pansy presented to the right means, "*I* have tender and pleasant thoughts"; presented to the left, it means, "*You* have tender and pleasant thoughts." These directions seem clear, but a question still remains as to point of view: is it the right or left of the giver, or of the receiver? An upright flower expresses a thought: an upside-down flower expresses the reverse meaning. Thus, a bachelor button given upright indicates "hope in love"; reversed, it means "no hope in love."

Carnation   Trefoil
"To cease to love is ceasing to exist." *(The Language of Flowers,* 1840)

When a flower is worn with apparel, its location can refine its meaning. The daffodil, which generally indicates "regard", means "regard for the mind or intelligence" when placed on the head and "regard for the heart, or love" when placed on the heart.

The condition of the plant suggested further nuances of

meaning. *Flora's Interpreter* states that a white rose means worth or "I am worthy of you", and a white rose withered means "I am in despair". The giver must hope that the flower stays in good condition until the message is perceived.

THE LANGUAGE OF PRESERVED PLANTS

Lucy Hooper, in her 1843 book, *The Lady's Book of Flowers and Poetry,* included a sizeable chapter on the "Management of Plants in Rooms" (a fashionable Victorian

---

FLOWER GAME.

HAVE a large bouquet ready; let each person draw from it a flower, and the meaning attached to it will typify the future consort's character. For example:—Say your bouquet for Spring consists of Violets, Hyacinths, Primroses, Daisies, Heart's-ease, Hawthorn, Daffodils; then the characters would be

Violet, modest; Hyacinth, playful; Dark Hyacinth, mournful; Primrose, simple, candid; Daisy, an early riser; Heart's-ease, kind, charitable, or thoughtful; Hawthorn, hopeful; Daffodil, daring.

For Summer.

Rose, loving; White Rose, secret and canny; Pink, haughty; Jasmine, elegant or amiable; Lily, pure; Mignonnette, clever; Tulip, proud, conceited; Stock, hasty; Mezereon, a flirt; Foxglove, deceitful; Myrtle, devoted; Laurel, brave; a Reed, musical; Hollyhock, ambitious; Marigold, rich; Poppy, lazy; Cornflower, extravagant; Dead Leaves, old; Geranium, stupid; Mimosa, nervous; Thistle, patriotic; Thyme, merry; Aster, changeable; Oak-leaf, hospitable.

The profession of the destined lover will be found thus:—Lily, a person of rank; Rose, an artist; Thistle, a Scotchman, and a soldier; Oak-leaf, a farmer; Laurel, a poet; Foxglove, a lawyer; Cypress, a doctor; Tulip, a freeholder; Passion-flower, a clergyman; Marigold, a merchant; Shamrock, an Irishman; Leek, a Welshman.

Of course the persons who draw the flowers are supposed to be ignorant of their meaning; or they may draw blindfolded.

In winter this game may be played with painted flower cards; painting a pack would be a pleasant home amusement; or dried flowers gummed on cards would answer perfectly well. The players then draw a card instead of a flower.

Taken from **The Language and Poetry of Flowers** *by an anonymous author, published in London by George Routledge and Sons.*

Carnation   Sweet Pea   Madwort   Heliotrope

To love is a pleasure, an happiness that intoxicates.

Carnation   Trefoil   End of Corn   Mercury

To cease to love is ceasing to exist; it is to have bought

Yew tree   Nightshade   White violet   Bugloss

this sad truth that innocence is a falsehood,

Myrtle   Acanthus   Madwort   Poppy

love an art, and happiness a dream.

A message of love using flower emblems
from *The Language of Flowers*, 1840.

practice), and preserving and drying fresh flowers were also popular endeavors. Pressed petals and snippets of leaves and stems were saved and classified by meaning so that, when fresh flowers were not available, flower pictures with silent significance could still be created. This

MODIFICATIONS

OF

THE FLOWER LANGUAGE.

IF a flower be given *reversed,* its original significa-tion is understood to be contradicted, and the oppo-site meaning to be implied.

A rosebud divested of its thorns, but retaining its leaves, conveys the sentiment, "I fear no longer; I hope:" thorns signifying fears, and leaves, hopes.

Stripped of leaves and thorns, the bud signifies, "There is nothing to hope or fear."

The expression of flowers is also varied by changing their positions. Place a marigold on the head, and it signifies "Mental anguish;" on the bosom, "Indif-ference."

When a flower is given, the pronoun *I* is understood by bending it to the right hand; *thou,* by inclining it to the left.

"Yes" is implied by touching the flower given with the lips.

"No," by pinching off a petal, and casting it away.

"I am" is expressed by a laurel-leaf twisted round the bouquet.

"I have," by an ivy-leaf folded together.

"I offer you," by a leaf of the Virginian Creeper.

To win—a sprig of parsley in the bouquet.

"May," or "I desire"—an ivy tendril round the bouquet.

An explanation of the rules of florigraphy from **The Poetry of Flowers.**

herbarium of plant meanings was suggested, along with the cultivation of flowers, as an appropriate pursuit.

This mode of communication may be carried even beyond the proper season of flowers, by the aid of an herbarium, in which flowers are preserved by simple pressure between the leaves of an album. Such an herbarium would be an ornament

Myrtle
"Love"

Sunflower
"False riches"

**"Your love is, like false riches,
not worth professing."**

to a parlour table, and would, moreover, encourage and facilitate the study of botany.

The Lady's Book of Flowers and Poetry, 1843

To Preserve Flowers and Plants: Place the specimens in a close, dark room; when the plants are nearly dry, press them, in small quantities enveloped in paper, till the oil appears on the surface, which you will know by its discoloring the paper; then do them up in clean paper bags, and they will retain their fragrance, color, and medicinal properties, for years.

Flora's Interpreter, 1833

THE MODERN LANGUAGE OF TUSSIE-MUSSIES

Love's language may be talked with these;
To work out choicest sentences
  No blossoms can be meeter;
And, such being used in Eastern bowers,
  Young maids may wonder if the flowers
  Or the meanings be the sweeter.
    Elizabeth Barrett Browning, 1806-1861

Today, interest in communicating in the language of herbs and flowers is increasing: we are once again drawn to know the sentiments represented by the fragrant and beautiful plants in our gardens. The editors of floral dictionaries of a century ago would undoubtedly be delighted that their florigraphy still flourishes and is learned and practiced by those who share the love of flowers with their Victorian ancestors.

Floral sentiments can be used to express wishes for many occasions. A gift of a tussie-mussie—an herb and flower "posy with a message"—expresses feelings in the language of plants with the beauty and fragrance of nature, recalling warm feelings and memories of a day when gifts were handmade and given from the heart. The lovely, tiny, fragrant bouquet makes a welcome gift which honors the recipient. A tussie-mussie can celebrate a holiday, birthday, wedding, friendship, recovery, achievement, new baby, or new home; it can say "Thank you", or simply "I love you": the list of possible messages is endless.

In eastern lands they talk in flowers,
  And they tell in a garland their loves and cares;
Each blossom that blooms in their garden bowers,
  On its leaves a mystic language bears.

The rose is the sign of joy and love,
  Young blushing love in its earliest dawn;
And the mildness that suits the gentle dove,
  From the myrtle's snowy flower is drawn.

Innocence shines in the lily's bell,
  Pure as a heart in its native heaven;
Fame's bright star and glory's swell,
  By the glossy leaf of the bay are given.

The silent, soft, and humble heart
  In the violet's hidden sweetness breathes;
And the tender soul that cannot part,
  A twine of evergreen fondly wreathes.

The cypress that darkly shades the grave,
  Is sorrow that mourns its bitter lot;
And faith that a thousand ills can brave,
  Speaks in thy blue leaves, forget-me-not.

Then gather a wreath from the garden bowers,
  And tell the wish of thy heart in flowers.

James G. Percival in
The Sentiment of Flowers, 1840

There are many ways to use the language of flowers in creations from the garden harvest. A nosegay made with carefully selected fresh or dried plants can convey a personal message. Florigraphy can be used to create potpourri or wreaths with a message as well as greeting cards and pictures with pressed leaves and flowers. Because many plants have more than one meaning, you can choose the one most appropriate to the message desired; but be sure to include a card that specifies the meanings chosen, in case (as is likely) the recipient is not well versed in florigraphy.

Interest is also reviving in wearing flowers as the Victorian ladies did in their daily lives. Tiny pin-on vases containing miniature bouquets are becoming popular, as is the practice of carrying tussie-mussies. We are more sensitive to nature around us; we appreciate the beauty and fragrance of the plants and seek to include them in our lives. Their fragrance lifts the spirit. By including flowers in your attire, you will become enchanted with this popular Victorian practice. A flower and a few sprigs of fragrant herbs can be slipped into a pocket, pinned to a collar, purse, or hat, tied in the hair, tucked into a waistband or buttonhole, or simply carried in hand.

Giving flowers is an even greater delight. The gift of a tussie-mussie is a gracious kindness and a token of love. Giving flowers and herbs is soothing and nurturing to the creator as well as the recipient. Treat yourself and those around you to a floral experience that will lift and refresh your spirit.

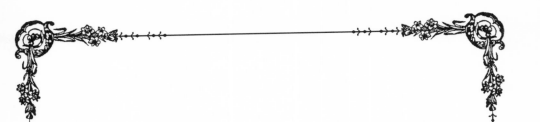

GODEY'S AMERICANIZED PARIS FASHIONS

Giving and receiving a tussie-mussie

FLORA'S LEXICON

Wallflower
"Faithful in misfortune"

Balsam   **Rose geranium**
"Impatience"   *"Preference"*

**"Be not impatient, but faithful in misfortune.
I give you the preference."**

Notes: Meanings for plants are listed chronologically, earliest assignment first; those created by the author (see page xi) are marked with an asterisk (*). Words in {braces} define the preceding word. Longer, explanatory paragraphs are quotations from floral dictionaries; their dates refer to books listed in Appendices under "Antique Floral Dictionaries". Black-and-white artwork is reproduced from Flora's Dictionary by E. W. Wirt, 1829; color art is from The Language of Flowers by Robert Tyas, 1869. Retouching of artwork was minimal; stains and discolorations of the aging pages are still visible.

ACACIA, *Robinia pseudacacia*: **PLATONIC LOVE.** The savages of North America have consecrated the Acacia to the genius of chaste love; their bows are made from the incorruptible wood of this tree, their arrows are armed with one of its thorns. These fierce children of the forest, whom nothing can subdue, conceive a sentiment of delicacy; perhaps what they are unable to express by words, but they understand the sentiment by the expression of a branch of blooming Acacia. The young savage, like the city coquette, understands this seducing language perfectly. The Acacia is a native of North America, and received its name from the botanist, Robin. *(1839)*

Acacia: friendship; chaste love

Acacia, rose: friendship

Acacia, white (common locust tree): elegance

Acacia, yellow: concealed love

Acanthus: the arts; emblem of genius

Adonis (pheasant's eye): sorrowful remembrances

Ageratum: aging not

Agrimony: gratitude; thankfulness

Allspice: compassion

Almond, flowering: hope; thoughtlessness; heedlessness

Aloe: religious superstition; bitterness, grief; acute sorrow, or affliction

Althea (hibiscus): consumed by love

**WHITE, YELLOW, AND
PURPLE ACACIA.**

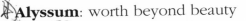

Alyssum: worth beyond beauty

AMARANTH, *Amaranthus*: **IMMORTALITY.** The amaranth is one of the latest gifts of autumn, and when dead its flowers retain their rich scarlet colour. The ancients have associated it with supreme honours, choosing it to adorn the brows of their gods. Poets have sometimes mingled its bright hue with the dark and gloomy cypress, wishing to express that their sorrows were combined with everlasting recollections. Homer tells us, that at the funeral of Achilles, the Thessalians presented themselves wearing crowns of amaranth. *(1839)*

Amaranth (prince's feather, celosia): unchangeable

Amaranth, globe: unchangeable; unfading love

Amaryllis: splendid beauty; "You are beautiful, but timid"; pride; haughtiness

Ambrosia: love returned

American cowslip: "You are my angel"

American starwort (Michaelmas daisy): cheerfulness in old age

Anemone (windflower, zephyr's flower): expectation, anticipation; abandon; love forsaken; sickness

Angelica: inspiration; magic; "Your love is my guiding star"

Apple: temptation

Apple blossom: preference; "Fame speaks him great and good"

Arbor vitae: "Live for me"; unchanging friendship; immortality; tree of life

The true and only tree is he
Who, like the Arbor-vitae tree,
Will bear our image on his heart.

Sir William Jones in
Flora's Interpreter, 1833

ASH, *Fraxinus*: **GRANDEUR.** There is a singular allegory in the Edda, which states that the gods hold their court under the shade of a miraculous ash, whose extensive branches shadow the whole surface of the earth; the top of the tree touches the heavens, and its roots descend to the regions of Pluto. An eagle constantly reposes on the

**ALTHEA, DWARF ALMOND, ALOE,
FLOS ADONIS OR PHEASANT'S EYE**

tree, to observe every thing, and a squirrel continually ascends and descends to make report. Beneath its roots flow two fountains. In the one wisdom is concealed, and in the other is found the knowledge of things to come. Three virgins are entrusted with the charge of this sacred tree, who ever remain under its branches to refresh the tree with these salutary waters, which, on falling back on the earth, form a dew that produces honey. This effect has been ingeniously compared to the results of inventive science. *(1839)*

✓**Aspen tree**: lamentation; excessive sensibility; groaning

Asphodel: "My regrets follow you to the grave"

Aster: variety; elegance; daintiness; patience

Auricula, scarlet: avarice {greed}; painting

Autumn crocus (colchicum): "I do not fear to grow old"

Azalea: romance; "I will always be true"

B

Baby's breath: gentleness; everlasting love

Bachelor buttons (cornflower): "I with the morning's love have oft made sport"; hope in love; single blessedness; celibacy

BALM, *Melissa officinalis*: **PLEASANTRY.** The generic name Melissa was no doubt given to this because it is pre-eminently a bee plant, an especial favourite with that ever active and industrious insect. Its flowers abound in honey. Its fresh leaves have the agreeable flavour of lemon. This fragrance is evanescent and not to be perceived in the dried plant. It used to be thought much of as a strengthener of the nerves, and as giving relief to the hypochondriac. An infusion of its leaves is now valued as a pleasant and cheering tea in the heat of the summer. *(1869)*

Balm (sweet balm, lemon balm, melissa): sympathy; social intercourse; pleasant company of friends; memories; a cure; "Don't misuse me"

Balm of Gilead: cure, healing

✓ **Balsam** (evergreen tree): friendship; "I miss you"

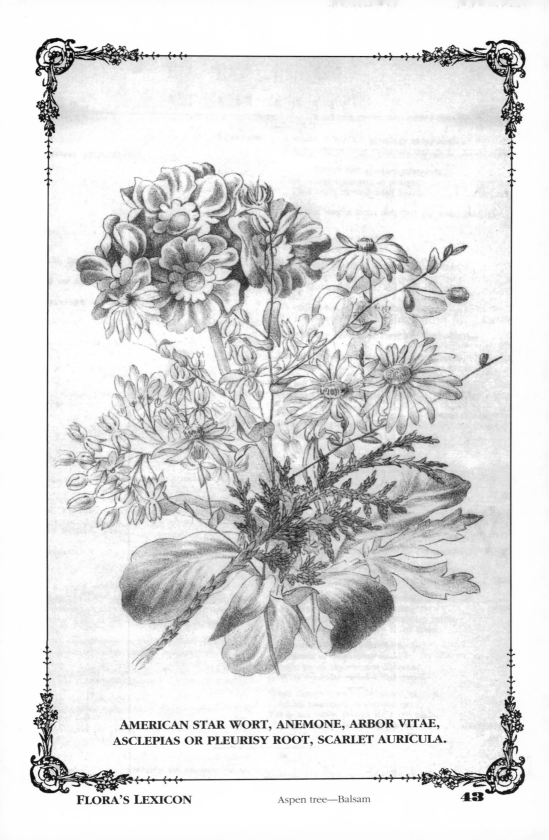

AMERICAN STAR WORT, ANEMONE, ARBOR VITAE, ASCLEPIAS OR PLEURISY ROOT, SCARLET AURICULA.

**ASPEN LEAVES, BACHELOR'S BUTTON, BALM,
RED AND YELLOW BALSAM, BARBERRY, SWEET BASIL.**

Balsam (yellow balsam, lady's slipper): impatience

Balsam, red (touch-me-not, impatiens): impatience, impatient resolves

Barberry: sharpness; sourness of temper

Basil, cinnamon: love of learning*

Basil, common: hate, "An enemy is near"

Basil, sweet: good wishes, best wishes; love or serious intentions

BAY, *Laurus nobilis*: GLORY. The Greeks and Romans consecrated crowns of laurel to every species of glory. They employed it to wreathe the brows of warriors and poets, of philosophers and statesmen, of vestals and emperors. This beautiful shrub grows abundantly in Delphos, on the shores of the river Peneus. There its aromatic branches of immortal verdure aspire to the height of the loftiest trees, and it is pretended that they possess a secret for averting thunder from the district where they grow.

The lovely Daphne was daughter of the river Peneus, but, preferring virtue to the love of the most eloquent of the gods, she fled to avoid the seducing magic of his words. Apollo pursued her, and when he was on the point of catching her, the nymph invoked her size and was changed into a laurel. *(1835)*

Bay: "My feelings will change only with death"

Bay, leaf: "I change but in dying"

Bay, wreath: reward of merit; glory; "I admire but cannot love you"

Bayberry: instruction

Bedstraw: hardness

Bee orchis (orchid): error

✓**Beech tree**: prosperity; grandeur; wedded love

Begonia: attention

Belladonna: silence; "Hush!"

BELLFLOWER, *Campanula rotundifolia*: **CONSTANCY.** The name of Bell-flower was never more appropriately bestowed than on this pretty, delicate plant, which has been imagined by some fanciful poets to ring out a peal of fairy music. *(1839)*

Belvidere (wild licorice, veronica): "I declare against you"

Berberry: tartness, sharpness

Bergamot (Monarda, bee balm): compassion, sympathy, consolation; sweet virtues

Betony (woolly betony, lamb's ears): surprise; healing

Bindweed: knots

✓**Birch tree**: neatness; gracefulness

Bird's-foot trefoil (milk vetch, lotus): revenge

Bladder-nut: frivolous amusement

Blue bell (wood hyacinth): delicacy; kindness

Bluebottle centaury (cornflower): delicacy

Bonus henricus (goosefoot, Good King Henry): goodness

Borage: bluntness; brusqueness; roughness of manners; "Your attentions only embarrass me"; courage

Bouquet of flowers: gallantry, politeness

Box: constancy; stoicism; constant love

Bramble: envy

Broom: humility; neatness

Bryony: prosperity; "Be my support"

Buckbean: calmness, repose

Bugloss: deceit; falsehood

BURDOCK, *Arctium lappa*: **IMPORTUNITY.** The Burdock is well known by all boys, to whom it is an inoffensive source of fun. They gather the seed-vessels, and throw them at their companions. The bristly hairs which cover the seed-vessels cling tenaciously to the dress, and require a little patience in detaching them. Thus the Burdock is a fitting emblem of that Importunity with which we are sometimes assailed by applicants, who seem determined not to take a refusal. It may also well be

**BAY LEAF, BEECH LEAF, BELVIDERE,
BLUE BOTTLE, BIRD'S-FOOT TREFOIL.**

regarded as such from its pertinacious resistance of attempts to extirpate its roots even from good soil. *(1869)*

Burdock burr: persistence; "I shall not be discouraged"; "Touch me not!"

Burnet: joy, a merry heart

BUTTERCUP, *Ranunculus*: **CHEERFULNESS.** Except the daisy, there is not a greater favourite than the Buttercup. Children of all ranks delight in it, and poets, calling to mind their early field pleasures, have not failed to speak of this wild flower, and have thus made a permanent record of the cheerfulness with which Buttercups inspired them. *(1869)*

Buttercup (king-cup): riches; a promise of future wealth; childishness

Butterfly flower: gaiety

Butterfly weed (milkweed): "Let me go"; "Stop your pestering"

Again I feel my heart is dancing,
With wildly-throbbing keen delight,
At this bright scene of King-cups dancing
Beneath the clear sun's golden light.

Again I pluck the little flower,
The first my childhood ever knew,
And think upon the place and hour
Where and when that first one grew;

And as I gaze upon its cup
Shining with burnished gold,
The faithful memory calls up
How many a friend beloved of old!

Anonymous in Tyas, 1869

CABBAGE: **PROFIT.** Formerly near Rome the fields were covered with cabbages, and those who cultivated them gained immense profits. Thence it is that the proverb is derived, *il fait chous gras,* he feathers his nest well; that is to say, he manages his affairs well, and everything turns to his advantage. *(1835)*

Cactus: "I burn"; warmth

Calendula (pot marigold): sacred affections; joy; remembrance; grief

Calla: feminine modesty

Calycanthus: benevolence

Camellia (Japan rose): pity; unpretending excellence; steadfast love; "My destiny is in your hands"

Camomile: energy in adversity; "May all your wishes come true"; "I admire your courage"

Campanula, bellflower: gratitude

Campanula, bluebell: constancy

Campanula, Canterbury bells: acknowledgment; "Grateful to a friend"

Campanula, harebell: submission; grief

Candytuft: indifference; <u>architecture</u>

Canna (flowering reed): confidence in heaven

CANTERBURY BELL, *Campanula medium*: GRATITUDE. This was a very fashionable plant some thirty years ago, and is still cultivated. It is used in Holland as an ornament to halls and staircases, and for placing before fireplaces in the summer. For this purpose it is planted in large pots, and is trained in such a manner as to cover a large surface, and continues to flower for two or three months in shady places. When in full flower it is a very magnificent plant, rising in a pyramidal shape, not unlike that of the towering pagoda. It may be trained to almost any shape, and we presume that on this account it has been made the emblem of gratitude. *(1839)*

Canterbury bell (campanula, bellflower): acknowledgment

Cape jasmine (gardenia): transport; ecstasy

Caraway: "We are betrayed"

Cardinal flower (lobelia): distinction

CARNATION, *Dianthus*: DISDAIN. We hope that disdain is as scarce among our countrywomen as the yellow carnation is in our native land. As disdainful people generally exact homage, and possess little amiability; so with this plant, it is the least beautiful and fragrant of its kind, yet requires continual care and attention. *(1839)*

Carnation: pride and beauty; pure and ardent love

Carnation, yellow: disdain

Carolina allspice (calycanthus): benevolence; gifts of love

Catchfly (silene, moss campion): pretended love

Catchfly, red: youthful love

Catchfly, white: "I fall into the trap laid for me"

Catnip: intoxication with love

✓ **Cedar tree** (red cedar): "I live for thee"; "Think of me"; incorruptibility; friendship; memory of love; strength

Celandine (swallow-wort): medicine

Celosia (prince's feather, amaranth): unchangeable; immortality

Cereus (night-blooming cereus): transient beauty

Chaste tree: coldness; chastity

Cherry tree: good education

Cherry tree blossom: spiritual beauty

Chervil: sincerity; love at first sight; warms old hearts

Chestnut: luxury

Chestnut tree: "Do me justice"

CHINA ASTER, *Aster chinensis*: **VARIETY OF CHARMS.**
Europe and America are indebted to the missionary, Father d'Incarville, for this beautiful various-coloured flower; he having first sent it to the "Jardin du Roe", at Paris, about 1730. At first it produced only simple flowers of one uniform colour; but, by cultivation, they became so doubled and quadrupled in form, and so varied in colour that it now forms one of the principal ornaments of the parterre, from July to November.

The Chinese, who have favoured us with this plant, make admirable use of it in decorating their gardens. To prepare them, they first raise the plants in pots; then separating the colours, they dispose them with such infinite art as to produce one splendid and harmonious whole. This effect is often increased by planting them near the side of a lake.

The China aster is made the emblem of variety; and owes its principal charms to a careful culture of the skilful gardener, who has surrounded its golden disks with every colour of the rainbow. So study produces an endless variety in the refinement of the human mind. Though majestic and brilliant, the China aster is not the imprudent rival of the rose, but succeeds it, and consoles us for its absence. *(1839)*

China aster (starwort): love of variety

China aster, double: "I partake of your sentiments"

China aster, single: "I will think of it"

China pink (Indian pink): aversion

Chives: usefulness; "Why do you weep?"

Christmas rose (hellebore): calumny {a misrepresentation intended to blacken another's reputation}; "Please relieve my anxiety"

CHRYSANTHEMUM, CHINESE, *Chrysanthemum indicum*: CHEERFULNESS. Cheerfulness is the best shield that can be found to lighten the strokes of adversity. This flower, that gives so much cheerfulness to the parterre, when nearly all the other children of Flora have withdrawn their smiles, is presented as the emblem of this enviable disposition, and of the loveliness which it adorns. *(1839)*

Chrysanthemum, Chinese: loveliness

Chrysanthemum, red: "I love"; "Alas, for my heart"

Chrysanthemum, white: truth; fidelity

Chrysanthemum, yellow: slighted love; jealousy; disdain

Cinnamon: wisdom

Cinquefoil (potentilla): beloved daughter

Clematis (virgin's bower): artifice {trickery}

Clematis, English: traveler's joy

Clematis, Virginiana: mental beauty; beauty of mind

Clove tree: dignity

Clover, four-leaf: "Be mine"; "You are lucky"

Clover, purple: providence

Clover, red: industry; "Think of me"

Cockscomb (crested amaranth): foppery {affection}; sillyness; singularity

Colchicum (autumn crocus, meadow saffron): "I do not fear to grow old"; "My best days are past"

Coltsfoot: maternal care; "Justice shall be done you"

COLUMBINE, *Aquilegia*: DESERTION. This graceful flower has long been a favourite inhabitant of the rustic flower border, and is commonly found in the open places of forests, or extensive woods. Why it has been made the emblem of folly it is difficult to say, some affirming that it is on account of the shape of its nectary, which turns over in similar manner to the caps of the ancient jesters; while others suppose it to be on account of the party colours which it generally assumes. *(1840)*

Columbine (granny's bonnet): folly

Columbine, purple: resolved to win

Columbine, red: anxious and trembling

Convolvulus (bind-weed, morning glory): uncertainty; worth sustained by affection

Convolvulus, field: captivation

Convolvulus, major: extinguished hopes

Convolvulus, minor: night

Convolvulus, white: humility

Coreopsis: "It is love at first sight"; always cheerful; gladness; cheerful smile

Coriander: hidden merit; "Your closeness is welcome"

Corn: riches

Cornelian cherry (dogwood): duration

Cornflower (bluebottle, bachelor button): delicacy; hope in love

Costmary (Bible-leaf): fidelity; sweetness

Cowslip, American: winning grace; "You are my angel"; "You are my divinity"; early joys

Crab blossom: ill nature

Cranberry: hardiness; cure for heartache

CROCUS, *Crocus vernus*: **PLEASURES OF HOPE.** The snowdrop is the emblem of consolation, reminding us that the season is approaching when blooming flowers will again deck the earth in beautiful profusion; with her attendant comes up the Crocus, which imparts to our hope of returning spring such emotions of pleasure, that it may well represent those agreeable sensations which pervade the mind when we see the purple, and golden, and violet-coloured flowers bursting through the earth, not seldom covered with snow, which gives additional zest to our gratification. Poets have at all times woven it into their verse. So poets, and all who delight in flowers, have felt a gush of pleasure when these bright things have first presented themselves in the parterre, a promise of the coming spring. *(1869)*

Crocus: cheerfulness; youthful gladness; mirth
Cross of Jerusalem: devotion; religious enthusiasm
Crown imperial: majesty, power; pride of birth
Crown of roses: reward of merit
Crown vetch: "May success crown your wishes"
Cuckoo-pink (ragged robin): ardour; dandy
Cyclamen: diffidence

CYPRESS, *Cupressus sempervirens*: **MOURNING.** The cypress is the universal emblem of mourning, and is the funeral tree in the eastern world, from the Persian Gulf to the Caspian Sea; it is also dedicated to the dead, from Mazanderan to Constantinople, as well as to the utmost bounds of China's fruitful shores.

Ovid gives us a traditional account of the mournful origin of the cypress tree, and we always find it devoted to mournful thoughts, or sad solemnities. Cyparissus, son of Telephus of Cea, was beloved by Apollo. Having killed the favourite stag of his friend, he grieved, pined, and, dying, was changed by Apollo into a cypress tree. Calmet describes it to be a tall, straight tree, having bitter leaves. The shade and smell were said to be dangerous; hence the Romans looked on it as a fatal tree, and made use of it at funerals. It is an evergreen; the wood is heavy, of rather a fragrant smell, is not liable to be attacked by insects, and does not speedily decay. Shakespeare says that cypress is the emblem of mourning; and we are told by Irving that, in

**DAHLIA, DAFFODIL,
RED DAISY, CYPRESS.**

Latium, on the decease of any person, a branch of cypress was placed before the door. *(1839)*

Cypress: despair; sorrow that mourns; death

D

Daffodil: chivalry; uncertainty; deceitful hope; regard

DAHLIA, *Dahlia superlua*: MY GRATITUDE EXCEEDS YOUR CARE. This favourite florist's flower, named in honour of Dahl, a Swedish botanist, is well known to every lover of Flora's subjects. It seems to have been imported into France about 1789, and its cultivation was nearly confined to that country until the peace of 1814. Then it was dispersed over Germany, Prussia, and Denmark; and found its way into England, where it soon became an object of great care and emulation, as well as a fruitful source of profit to the florist.

The dahlia needs but little care after planting, yielding an abundance of flowers; but the amateur who has a genuine taste for beauty in his favourites, will, if he can possibly devote the necessary time to such a purpose, so train his plants, and reduce the number of their incipient bloom, as to produce the finest flowers which they are capable of bearing. And in so doing he will realize an enhanced pleasure in their possession, not fearing that they will complain of his negligence, in his absence, in the management of his parterre. On the contrary, when he shall have returned he will receive their gratulations on the beauty of his flowers, and on the rich reward he has secured in such a charming display of lasting bloom. *(1869)*

Dahlia: forever thine; elegance and dignity; instability

DAISY: I WILL THINK OF IT. In the time of chivalry, when a lady would neither accept nor reject the vows of her lover, she ornamented her forehead with a wreath of field daisies, which expressed, "I will think of it." *(1840)*

Daisy, red: beauty unknown to the possessor

Daisy, white: innocence; simplicity; "I share your sentiments"; "I will think of it"

DANDELION, *Leontodon taraxacum*: ORACLE. This globe of down is also the Oracle to every incipient lover of either sex. The youth not yet in his 'teens, meeting with one of them, begins to tempt his fate. He plucks the seed-stem from the plant, and puffs away the feathered sphere, alternately saying, "She loves me!", "She loves me not!", thinking of the pretty face and sparkling eyes which enchanted his throbbing heart at the last juvenile party. Then, according as one of these sentences is uttered as the last sphere leaves its native station, so is the answer to his anxious inquiry. The response is somewhat like those of the Delphic Oracle, very ambiguous, and capable of being interpreted as the inquirer desires. So he breathes gently or fiercely, softly or sharply, lest the response should dissipate the fond illusion which is adding a new and delicious charm to his young life. *(1869)*

Dandelion: coquetry {a flirtatious act or attitude}; absurdity; "I find your presumptions laughable"

Daphne (February daphne, mezereon): timidity; sweets to the sweet

Darnel: vice

Dead leaves: melancholy, sadness

Delphinium: heaven

Dew plant (fig-marigold, Mary-bud): a serenade

Dianthus: Mother's love; emblem for Mother's Day

The Decision of the Flower

And with scarlet poppies around, like a bower,
 The maiden found her mystic flower;
"Now, gentle flower, I pray thee tell
 If my lover loves me, and loves me well;
So may the fall of the morning dew
 Keep the sun from fading thy tender blue.

Now I number the leaves for my lot —
 He loves me not: he loves me: he loves me not —
He loves me: yes, thou last leaf, yes —
 I'll pluck thee not for that last sweet guess!
He loves me!": "Yes," a dear voice sigh'd,
 And her lover stands by Margaret's side.

Miss Landon in *Flora's Lexicon*, 1839

DICTAMNUS: FIRE. Fraxinella, the specific name, was given to this plant because its leaves closely resemble those of the Ash (Fraxinus). If you rub the plant with your fingers, it will emit a lemon scent; if you bruise it, the fragrance will be balsamic. The footstalks of the flowers are supposed to contain this fine scent. They are studded with glands of a rusty red, which exude a resinous or viscous fluid. This fluid exhales in vapour, and may be seen to take fire in dark places. It is alleged that when the day has been very hot and dry, and the evening damp,

FIR, FOX GLOVE, FUCHSIA,
APPLE GERANIUM, CRANE'S BILL GERANIUM.

this exhalation is so inflammable as to ignite if a lighted bougie {wax candle} be brought near the plant. *(1869)*

Dill: to lull; good spirits

Dittany (dittany of Crete): birth

Dodder: baseness

Dog rose: simplicity

OGWOOD, the Cornelian cherry, *Cornus sanguinea*: DURATION. The wood of this tree is said to be as hard as horn (cornu); hence its generic name. Virgil tells us that it was used in the manufacture of implements of war. The wood is applied to a variety of purposes. It is called Dogwood. As a shrub, it is a good emblem of Hardness and Duration; for in plantations where the lower branches have perished, there, even under the drip of trees, this will flourish and fill up the vacant spaces.

The Greeks worshiped Apollo, to whom they consecrated this tree, because he presided over works of talent. It is, therefore, an emblem worthy of adoption by all who are determined to cultivate literature, oratory, and poetry; since, if they would win the laurel leaf, it must be by patient enduring labour, in study and in persistent reflection. *(1869)*

Dogwood (Cornelian cherry): "I am perfectly indifferent to you"; love undiminished by adversity; durability

Dragon plant: snare

Ebony: blackness

GLANTINE, *Rosa rubiginosa*: POETRY. The Eglantine, or Sweet-briar Rose, is regarded as being specially the flower of poets. In the floral games it is awarded as the prize for the best production in praise of the pleasures of study, and the charms of oratory. But not only is it the Poet's flower, for, thriving in every situation, and universally admired and appreciated, both for its permanent fragrance, and the beauty and elegance of its simple flowers in their season, it is a most fitting emblem of poetry. Like it, genuine poetry appeals to the affections and sings of the feelings belonging to our common humanity and is fully appreciated, and therefore fully delighted in, as well, by the cottager who becomes acquainted with it by hearing, as by crowned heads who read it at leisure in the splendid palaces.

Our sweet Eglantine scatters its rich fragrance over, and beautifies the hedgerows and gardens of our transatlantic brethren. *(1869)*

Eglantine (European sweet briar): "I wound to heal"

Elder (elderberry, European elder): compassion; zealousness

Elecampane: woe, sorrow, "I cry for you"

Elm: dignity

Elm, American: patriotism

Enchanter's night shade: witchcraft; fascination

Endive: frugality

English daisy (bellis): beauty and innocence

EVENING PRIMROSE, *Oenothera*: **INCONSTANCY.** It is uncertain when this beautiful flower was first introduced into England, though we know that it was brought from Virginia to Padua in the year 1619. It is a general favourite with our poets, who give it a very different character to that we have assigned to it in floral language. We presume that it has been made the emblem of Inconstancy on account of the transient duration of its flowers. It opens between six and seven o'clock in the evening. *(1839)*

Evergreen: poverty

Evergreen thorn: solace in adversity

Everlasting (baby's breath, strawflower, statice): never ceasing remembrance

Everlasting (strawflower): always remembered

Everlasting pea: lasting pleasure

F

FENNEL, *Anethum foeniculum*: **STRENGTH.** The gladiators in training for exhibition used to mix Fennel with their food, for the purpose of stimulating their energies. Successful gladiators were crowned with a garland of Fennel, after the sports were concluded. It is now used by us for culinary purposes, giving flavour to sauces served with salmon and mackerel. It forms a pretty garnish to these fish. The seeds are a strong carminative, and great quantities are annually imported from France for use in medicine. *(1869)*

Fennel: worthy of all praise; flattery

Fern: sincerity; fascination

Feverfew (fever root): delay; fire, warmth; protection; "I reciprocate your affection"; "You light up my life"*

Field daisy: "I will think of it"

Field lily: humility

Fig: longevity; argument

Fig tree: prolific

Filbert: reconciliation

Fir: time

Fir tree: elevation

Flax: domestic industry; "I feel your kindness"; appreciation; fate

FORGET-ME-NOT, *Myosotis palustris*: **FORGET ME NOT.** Though every one knows why this pretty flower is used to express the wish, "Forget me not", we must here repeat the story: Two lovers, on the eve of marriage, were walking on the banks of the Danube. A flower, blue as the deepest sky, swung upon the waves, which seemed ready to bear it away. The young lady admired its beautiful colour, and bewailed its impending destiny. The affianced bridegroom leaped into the stream, seized the blooming stem, and sunk engulfed in the flowing waters. It is said that, with a last effort, he threw the flower on the bank, and at the moment of his disappearance forever, cried out, "Love me; forget me not!" *(1869)*

Forget-me-not (mouse-ear): true love; remember me

Foxglove: a wish; insincerity; stateliness; silence; South

Frankincense: the incense of a faithful heart; gladness

Fraxinella (dictamnus): fire

Fuchsia (love-lies-a-bleeding): "The ambition in my love thus plagues itself"; "Your charms are engraven on my heart"; confiding love; taste

Fumitory (wee folk's stockings): hatred

Gardenia (cape jasmine): transport ecstasy; secret untold love, "I love you in secret"; joy, "I am too happy"

Garlic: charm against evil; "I can't stand you"

GATHERED FLOWERS: WE DIE TOGETHER. It is well known how soon a mass of flowers decomposes the air, and renders it unfit for respiration, producing sickness and death. This fact has suggested to a German writer, Freiligrath, a touching sketch, which he calls "The Revenge of the Flowers".

"Returning from a botanical excursion, two young girls enter their home, close the windows, lie down and fall asleep. At their feet, in a basket, is seen the flowers which they have collected. How indiscreet! Where is their mother? Who will warn them of the danger which surrounds them? Already the air is being decomposed, the atmosphere of the small apartment is heavy and unfit to breathe, and the youthful maidens weighed down by it writhe about unconsciously on their couch. Suddenly, from amid the basket of flowers, rise up the spirits of the narcissus and the tuberose! They appear as two light nymphs dancing and whirling about, meanwhile chanting ominous words: "Young maidens! young maidens! why have you deprived us of life? Nature gives us but a day, and you have shortened it! Oh! how sweet was the dew! how radiant the sun! and yet we must die! But we will be avenged." Thus chanting, the two nymphs, continually whirling about and bewailing their fate, draw near the young maidens' couch, and breathe over their faces their poisonous exhalations. Poor children! Mark their livid cheeks! their pale lips! their arms closely interwoven! Alas! their heart has ceased to beat; they no longer breathe the breath of life; they are dead together. The flowers are avenged!" *(1869)*

SILVER LEAVED GERANIUM,
GILLYFLOWER, GOLDENROD.

Gentian: virgin pride; "I love you best when you are sad"

Geranium, apple-scented leaf: present preference

Geranium, crane's bill: envy

Geranium, fish: disappointed expectation

Geranium, grey leaf: recall

Geranium, ivy: "Your hand for the next quadrille?"; bridal favor

Geranium, lemon-scented leaf: tranquility of mind; unexpected meeting

Geranium, mourning: despondency

Geranium, nutmeg-scented leaf: an expected meeting

Geranium, oak leaf: "Lady, deign to smile"; true friendship

Geranium, peppermint-scented leaf: cordial feelings*

Geranium, rose-scented leaf: preference

G ERANIUM, SCARLET: FOLLY. Madame de Stael was always angry when any one tried to introduce into her society a mindless man. One day, however, a friend of hers risked the introduction of a young Swiss officer of very pleasing figure. The lady, misled by his appearance, became animated, and uttered a thousand pleasant remarks to the newcomer, who at first seemed dumb with surprise and admiration. But, since he listened in silence for an hour, she began to doubt the cause of his conduct, and all at once addressed him with such direct questions, that it was quite necessary that he should answer. Alas! the unfortunate fellow could reply with nothing but foolish nonsense. M. de Stael then turned away, vexed at her loss of pains and mental effort, and, addressing herself to her friend, said, "Truly sir you are like my gardener, who thought to give me a treat by bringing me this morning a pot of Geraniums; but I tell you that I sent the flower away, desiring him never to let me see it again." "Ah! why so?" asked the young man in astonishment. "It is, sir, since you wish to know it, because the Geranium is a flower well clad in scarlet: so long as we look at it, it pleases the eye; but when we press it lightly, it emits a disagreeable odour." While saying this, the lady rose and went out, leaving, as we may well imagine, the cheeks of the young officer as red as his regimentals, which were the colour of the flower to which he had been compared.

The scarlet Geranium is a most pleasing object in beds on our lawns, displaying its masses of brilliant flowers to great advantage in the later Summer months. *(1869)*

Geranium, scarlet: stupidity

Geranium, scented leaf: gentility; preference

Geranium, silver-leaved {colored-leaved geranium, leaf color green and white} (grey): recall

German iris: ardour; flame

Germander (speedwell): facility; joy; faithfulness

GILLYFLOWER, *Cherianthus Incanus*: LASTING BEAUTY. The gillyflower, less graceful than the rose, less superb than the lily, has a splendour more durable. Constant in its benefits, it offers to us, all the year, its beautiful red and pyramidal flowers, which always diffuse an agreeable odour. The finest gillyflowers are red; they derive their name from their colour, which rivals in brilliancy the far-famed purple of Tyre. White, violet, and variegated gillyflowers have also their charms. This beautiful flower may be said to grow in our parterres, like a blooming and lively beauty, who scatters health around her; health, that chief of blessings, without which there can be neither happiness nor lasting beauty. *(1839)*

Gillyflower (clove pink): bonds of affection; "She is fair"; unfading beauty

Gladiolus: strength of character; ready armed

Glasswort: pretension

Globe amaranth: immortality; unfading love

Glory flower, crimson: glorious beauty

Gloxinia: a proud spirit

Glycine: "Your friendship is pleasing and ageeable to me"

Goat's rue: reason

Goldenrod: encouragement; precaution; indecision, "Allow me time to decide"

Good King Henry (goose-foot): goodness

Gorse: cheerfulness in adversity; anger

Grape, wild: charity; mirth

**WILD GRAPE, GRASS, HAWTHORN,
YELLOW AND PURPLE HEART'S EASE.**

GRASS, *Gramen*: **UTILITY.** It will be admitted that what is the most useful, is in nature the most common; and of all vegetable productions, what is there more common than grass? It clothes the earth with a verdant carpet, and it yields food, nay, it "grows for the cattle," in obedience to the Creator's word. *(1839)*

Grass: submission; usefulness

Harebell (campanula, bluebell): grief; delicate and lonely as this flower; submission

Hawthorn: hope

Hazel: reconciliation; peace

HEARTSEASE, *Viola tricolor*: **THINK OF ME.** The tints of this flower are scarce less varied than the names that have been bestowed upon it. That of pansy is a corruption of the French name, *pensie*, thought.
Lehigh Hunt introduces the heart's-ease into his verses:

> *The garden's gem,*
> *Heart's-ease, like a gallant bold,*
> *In his cloth of purple and gold.*

Phillips observes that the most brilliant purples of the artist appear dull when compared to that of the pansy; our richest satins and velvets coarse and unsightly by a comparison of texture; and as to delicacy of shading, it is scarcely surpassed by the bow of Iris itself. *(1839)*

Heartsease, yellow and purple (Johnny-jump-up): "Forget me not"; happy thoughts; the Valentine herb

Heartsease, purple: "You occupy my thoughts"

Heartsease, wild: love in idleness

Heath: solitude

Heather: beauty in solitude; admiration

Heather, white: good luck

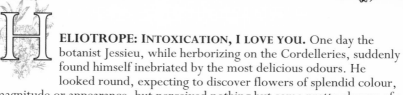

HELIOTROPE: **INTOXICATION, I LOVE YOU.** One day the botanist Jessieu, while herborizing on the Cordelleries, suddenly found himself inebriated by the most delicious odours. He looked round, expecting to discover flowers of splendid colour, magnitude or appearance, but perceived nothing but some pretty clumps of a gentle green, from the bottom of which little capsules, of faded blue colour, were detaching themselves. These little bushes are about six feet high, and he observed that the flowers with which they were bespangled gently turned towards the sun, which they seemed to regard with love. Struck with this appearance, he gave the name of heliotrope to the flower, from the Greek word signifying "to turn" and "sun." The learned botanist, charmed with his acquisition, eagerly collected some of the seeds of this plant, and sent them to the Jardin du Roi, where they have succeeded. The fair sex, in their enthusiasm, made a floral pet of this flower. They placed it in vases of the most precious materials, christened it the "flower of love," and regarded with contempt the gift of any bouquet of flowers from which their favourite was excluded. It was therefore under female patronage that the Peruvian heliotrope, after being cultivated the first time in Paris, in 1740, has made its fortune in the world, and triumphantly completed the tour of Europe. One day a very charming woman, who doted passionately on the heliotrope, was asked what she could see in this dull and sombre looking plant to justify so much admiration? "Because," replied she, " the heliotrope's perfume is to my parterre what the soul is to beauty, refinement to love, and love to youth." *(1835)*

Heliotrope (cherry-pie): devotion; intoxicated with pleasure; devoted affection; faithfulness; eternal love

Hellebore: calumny {false accusation}; slander

Hemlock: "You will be my death"

Henbane: fault

HEPATICA, *Hepatica triloba*: **CONFIDENCE.** This is a great favourite in the flower border, not only on account of the various colours it displays, but their many shades. The leaves are so formed as to bear a striking resemblance to the lobes of the liver, whence its generic name. It blooms from February to April; and when it spreads forth its pretty petals, the gardener knows that the earth is in a genial state, and that he may with confidence sow his seeds. *(1869)*

Hibiscus (Althea, China rose): delicate beauty; consumed by love

Hickory: glory

Hoarhound (horehound): frozen kindness; health

Holly: "Am I forgotten?"; domestic happiness; foresight; good wishes

HOLLYHOCK, *Alcaea rosea*: FRUITFULNESS. All the world knows this superb plant, which is supposed to be a native of China, or rather of Syria, whence it is said to have been brought to Europe in the time of the crusades. From its extreme fecundity in the production of flowers it has been made the emblem of fruitfulness. Pliny mentions it as a rose growing on stalks like the mallow; and Miller states that he received seeds from Istria, where they were gathered in the fields; these seeds produced only single red flowers, while seeds received from Madras yielded plants with double flowers of a variety of colours.

There are few flowers that contribute more to the embellishment of large gardens that the hollyhock, although their hardy nature and easy propagation have rendered them so common that they are much less regarded by the generality of florists than they deserve. *(1839)*

Hollyhock (rose mallow): ambition; fecundity {fruitful in offspring}; foresight

Hollyhock, white: female ambition

Honesty (money-plant, moonwort, satin flower): sincerity; fascination; honesty; money-in-both-pockets

Honeyflower: "Speak low if you speak love"; "I have lost all"

Honeysuckle: "I would not answer hastily"

Honeysuckle, coral: the color of my fate; fidelity; ties of love; bonds of love; generous and devoted affection; a sweet disposition

Honeysuckle, wild (woodbine): generous and devoted love; inconstancy: likely to change frequently without reason

Hop: injustice

Horehound: frozen kindness; health

Horse-chestnut: luxury

Houseleek: vivacity

Houstonia: content

Hoya: sculpture

Hyacinth: jealousy; play, game; sport

Hyacinth, blue: constancy

Hyacinth, purple: sorrow

HYDRANGEA, *Hydrangea hortensis*: YOU ARE COLD. This plant was brought from China about eighty years ago. It is highly valued for its great profusion of elegant flowers, which are by nature of a rosy tinge. By culture, under some circumstances, they become blue, an effect which florists seem to aim at. The plant is very ornamental in large rooms and halls; and when the flowers are blue the whole plant has a cold appearance, whence it has been thought to be emblematic of a coquette, who, devoid of any estimable qualities, seeks to please only by attention to her toilet. *(1869)*

Hydrangea: a boaster; heartlessness; "You are heartless"

Hyssop: cleanliness; sacrifice

ICE PLANT: YOUR LOOKS FREEZE ME. The leaves of this singular plant are covered with transparent vesicles full of water. When the plant is in the shade it appears covered with dew; exposed to the rays of the sun it appears covered with frozen crystals that give it great brilliancy. *(1835)*

Ice plant: rejected addresses; an old beau; coldness

Iceland moss: health

Impatiens (balsam, yellow balsam): impatience

Indian cress, three-coloured: resignation

Indian jasmine: separation

Ipomoea: "I attach myself to you"

**RUSH LEAVED JONQUIL,
IRIS, IVY, LABURNUM.**

IRIS: **MESSAGE.** This plant is supposed to have been named after Juno's attendant, because its colours are similar to those bestowed on the messenger of that goddess, by poets and mythological writers. Iris is usually portrayed as descending from a rainbow; and the eye of heaven (Plutarch says that is the meaning of the word Iris) is not more variegated than the flower that has been honoured by her name. *(1839)*

Iris: "I have a message for you"; my compliments
Iris, blue: message, messenger
Iris, red: a flame; "I burn"
Iris, yellow: flame of love

IVY, *Hedera*: **FRIENDSHIP.** Faithful love secures with a branch of ivy the quickly fading roses which adorn the brow. Friendship has chosen for its device an ivy which clothes a fallen tree. In Greece, the altar of Hymen was surrounded with ivy, a sprig of which was presented by the priest to a new-married spouse, as a symbol of an indissoluble knot. Ingratitude has sometimes been represented by ivy, as when it attaches itself to a young tree it confines the stem, and consequently prevents the free circulation of the sap. The author of a French work has repelled this calumny. The ivy appears to him to be the emblem of eternal friendship; he says, "Nothing is able to separate the ivy from the tree around which it has once entwined itself; it clothes the object with its own foliage in that inclement season when its black boughs are covered with hoar frost; the companion of its destinies, it falls when the tree is cut down. Death itself does not detach it, but it continues to decorate with its constant verdure the dry trunk it had chosen as its support. *(1839)*

Ivy: matrimony, wedded love, fidelity, marriage; constancy; "I engage you for the next dance"

Jacob's ladder: "Come down from your pedestal"

J ASMINE, WHITE, *Jasminum officinale*: AMIABILITY. Though born beneath a summer sky, and nourished by a kindlier soil than ours, yet the pure, the fragrant, the modest, maidenly Jasmine has become unto us as an old familiar friend, and is now as well known, and as frequently seen climbing round the cottage-porch, as our own luscious Honey-suckle. *(1839)*

Jasmine: "I attach myself to you"
Jasmine, white: amiability; sensuality
Jasmine, yellow: grace and elegance
Jasmine, Carolina yellow: separation
Johnny-jump-up (heartsease): happy thoughts

J ONQUIL, *Narcissus jonquilla*: DESIRE. This species of narcissus is distinguished from others by its rush-like foliage; hence its name, derived from juncus, rushy. It is more fragrant than any other species of the plant, and is frequently found too strong for moderate-sized rooms. It flowers well in water, is of great beauty, and very popular. *(1839)*

Jonquil: "I desire a return of affection"
Juniper: asylum, protection

K

K ENNEDIA, ELEGANT SCARLET, *Kennedia coccinea elegans*: MENTAL BEAUTY. This is a charming variety of the Kennedia Coccinea, and deserves the most extensive cultivation. It grows delicate, and is well suited for climbing up a pillar in a conservatory, where it will flower to perfection. Its rare delicacy and beauty render it a suitable emblem of Mental Beauty. *(1839)*

King-cup (buttercup): desire of riches; "I wish I was rich"

Laburnum: pensive beauty

Lady's mantle: comfort, protection

Lady's slipper (garden balsam): capricious {impulsive, unpredictable} beauty

Lantana: rigor; sharpness

Larch: boldness

Larkspur: lightness; haughtiness; levity; ardent attachment; swiftness

Larkspur, pink: fickleness

Laurel (bay laurel): treachery; glory

Laurel, mountain (calico bush): "Virtue makes her charming"; ambition

Laurustinus (viburnum): a token; "I die if neglected"

L**AVENDER**, *Lavandula spica*: **DISTRUST.** A notion prevailed in days of yore that the Asp, a most dangerous kind of viper, delighted chiefly to dwell under the Lavender plant; which on that account was always approached with Distrust. It yields an agreeable scent by distillation, and its dried stems and leaves and flowers supply a most pleasing means of perfuming many domestic articles. Miss Strickland says its "fragrance never dies." *(1869)*

Lavender: acknowledgment; suspicion; devotion; constant personal attention; luck; loyalty

Lemon: zest

Lemon balm (balm, sweet balm, melissa): social intercourse; pleasant company of friends; memories; a cure; "Don't misuse me"

Lemon blossom: discretion

Lemon verbena: enchantment; delicacy of feeling; "You have bewitched me"

LETTUCE, *Lactuca sativa*: **COLDNESS.** This well-known garden plant is the suitable emblem of coldness, but coldness most agreeable, since nothing is more delicious to the palate than the crisp, juicy heart of the Lettuce in the hot days of summer. *(1869)*

Lettuce: cold-hearted

Lichen (tall moss, tree moss): solitude

Lilac, Persian: forsaken

Lilac, purple: first emotions of love; fastidiousness

Lilac, white: youth; youthful innocence

Lily: majesty; splendor

Lily, day: coquetry; playful gaiety

Lily, white: purity and sweetness, purity and beauty

Lily, yellow: falsehood, untruth

LILY OF THE VALLEY, *Convallaria majalis*: **RETURN OF HAPPINESS.** This greatly admired flower loves the recesses of our valleys, the shade of oak-trees, and the banks of flowing streams.

From the early days of May she unfolds her ivory flowers, and scatters their fragrance around. Then the nightingale forsakes our hedges and our thickets, and seeks in the forest glade a companion, a loneliness and an echo which responds to his song; led by the perfume of the Lily of the Valley, the lovely bird soon finds an agreeable asylum; there he takes up his abode, where he celebrates, in most melodious notes, solitude and love, and the flower which, in each succeeding Spring, proclaims to him the Return of Happiness.

Wiffen expresses his admiration of the Lily of the Valley:

Spring's darling, nature's pride, the sylvan's queen.

Who does not promptly join in this? What flowers do we look for so frequently, so eagerly, as for those of the Lily of the Valley which attend, if they do not foretell, the return of the happy days of Spring and Summer, which follow the dreariness and gloom of winter? *(1869)*

Lily of the valley: delicacy, delicate simplicity; purity; "Let us make up" *To Victorians 'the return of happiness'*

Lime tree: conjugal love

Linden tree: conjugal love; matrimony

Liver-wort: confidence

**PURPLE AND WHITE LILAC,
WHITE LILY, LILY OF THE BARREN.**

Lobelia, scarlet (cardinal flower): malevolence; arrogance; distinction

Locust tree: affection beyond the grave; by chance

LONDON PRIDE, *Saxifraga umbrosa*: FRI and almost universal border plant is a species received the name also of none-so-pretty; and attention, we shall acknowledge that its pretti which are painted with so much delicacy, fully deserve Notwithstanding its beauty, it has been made the emble frivolous sentiment, for a lover would think it an insult present her with a nosegay of its flowers. *(1839)*

London pride: light and frivolous sentime

LOTOS, *Lotus*: ESTRANGED LOVE. A favourite ancients, who frequently refer to it in their po The definition of Lotos in the Greek Lexicon, this: "A tree whose fruit is so sweet that foreig of it, forget their own country": whence the proverb, to have eaten of the Lotos, is applied to those who prefer a foreign country to their own. Its flower is the emblem of estranged love; its leaf of recantation. *(1839)*

Lotus flower: silence

Lotus leaf: recantation

Lovage: hidden virtues; cleanliness

Love-in-a-mist: perplexity; "I am perplexed"

Love-lies-a-bleeding (tassel flower, kiss-me-over-the-garden-gate): hopeless, not heartless

Lozenge-leaved bobon: concealment

LUCERN, *Medicago sativa*: LIFE. Lucern occupies the same ground for a long period, but when it forsakes it, it is for ever. On this account it has been made the emblem of life. Nothing is more charming than a field of lucern in full flower. It seems spread before our eyes like a carpet of green and violet. Cherished by the husbandman, it yields him an abundant crop without much care; and, when mowed, it springs up again. The cattle rejoice at its appearance; it is a favourite plant with the sheep; and the goat receives it as a delicacy; while the horse also eats it with avidity. *(1839)*

Lunaria (moonwort): forgetfulness

Lupine: imagination; dejection, sorrow; voraciousness

M

MADDER, *Rubia tinctorum*: **CALUMNY.** This plant is well known as yielding a red and scarlet dye for clothiers and calico-printers. It is for the most part imported from Holland, though at one time it was cultivated here under difficulties. Sheep and animals feeding upon it have their milk and bones dyed by it; and when they feed alternately upon this and grass, the bones are dyed in concentric circles. Sheep's teeth when eating it, are tinged as with the blood of a victim, which imputes a sanguinary disposition to an animal the most simple; thus malice will sometimes profit by a false appearance to calumniate innocence itself. *(1869)*

Madwort, rock: tranquility

Magnolia: love of nature; high souled

Magnolia, swamp: perseverance

Mallow: sweet disposition

Maidenhair: discretion

Manchineel: duplicity; falsity

Mandrake: rarity

Maple tree: reserve, retirement

MARYGOLD, *Calendula*: **INEQUITUDE.** Madame Lebrun, in one of her charming pictures, has represented grief as a young man pale and languishing; his head appears to be bowed down by the weight of a garland of marygolds. All the world knows this gilded flower, which has been made the emblem of distress of mind; or rather, we should say of that inequitude which is caused by uncertainty as to

**MOCK ORANGE, MOSS, MULLEIN,
MYRTLE, CANDLEBERRY MYRTLE.**

the sentiments of the one we love with a peculiar affection. The lover longs to know whether there be a reciprocal feeling in the heart of his mistress towards himself, or whether he has been buoying himself up with false hope. We verily believe that there are few who would not prefer to receive the dread intelligence that his suit is rejected, than remain in this uncertain state. *(1839)*

The yellow flower was sacred to Venus, and highly prized by the ancients. It has been devoted by Catholics to the Virgin Mary (Mary's Gold). *(1833)*

Marigold: cruelty; grief, sorrow; joy; remembrance; affections; pain; chagrin; the friendship flower

Marigold, French: jealousy

Marjoram, sweet: blushes; maidenly innocence; "Your passion sends blushes to my cheeks"

Marjoram, wild: joy and happiness

Marsh mallow: humanity; beneficence

Marvel of Peru (mimosa, sensitive plant): timidity

Meadow anemone: sickness

Meadow saffron: "My best days are past"

Meadowsweet: inutility; uselessness

Mezereon (daphne): desire to please; emblem of coquetry

MICHAELMAS DAISY, *Aster tradescanti*: AFTERTHOUGHT. The Michaelmas Daisy begins to display her bloom, when all other flowers are becoming rare. It is an After-thought of Flora, who bestows upon us a parting smile on her quitting our parterres. *(1869)*

Michaelmas daisy (American starwort): cheerfulness in old age; farewell

MIGNONETTE, *Reseda odorata*: YOUR QUALITIES SURPASS YOUR CHARMS. The odour exhaled by this little flower is thought by some to be too powerful for the house; but even those persons, we presume, must be delighted with the fragrance which it throws from the balconies into the streets of the city, giving something like a breath of garden air to the "close-pent man," whose avocations will not permit a ramble beyond the squares of the fashionable part of the town. *(1839)*

Mignonette: "Your qualities surpass your loveliness"

Milk vetch: "Your presence softens my pain"

Milkwort: hermitage

Mimosa: sensitiveness

Mignonette

Now look ye on the plain and modest guise
Of yon unlovely flower: unlovely?: no —
Not beautiful, 'tis true: not touch'd with hues
Like her's we late have gazed on; but so rich
In precious fragrance is that lovely one,
So loved for her sweet qualities, that I
Should woo her first amid a world of flower;
For she is like some few beloved ones here,
Whom eyes, perchance, might slightingly pass o'er,
But whose true wisdom, gentleness, and worth,
Unchanging friendship, ever-faithful love,
And countless minor beauties of the mind,
Attach our hearts in deep affection still.

Twamley, in *Flora's Lexicon*, 1839

MINT: GRIEF. In Holstein the youths carry to funerals a branch of mint, as a mark of grief. In India the lemon is consecrated to grief, the women who burn themselves on the death of their husbands walk to the funeral pyre with lemons in their hands. *(1835)*

Mint: homeliness, homely virtue; wisdom; eternal refreshment; "Find a spouse of your own age and background"; "Don't make such a to-do about small things"

Mistletoe: "I overcome everything"; parasite; "I surmount difficulties"; "I rise above all"

Mock orange: counterfeit; disappointment; deceit; memory; fraternal affection

Monthly rose: ever fair

Moonwort (lunaria): forgetfulness

Monkshood (aconite): deceit; dislike; "Your attentions are unwelcome"

Morning glory (convolvulus): worth sustained by affection; affection; bonds

Moschatel (musk plant): weakness

Money wort

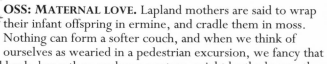

MOSS: **MATERNAL LOVE.** Lapland mothers are said to wrap their infant offspring in ermine, and cradle them in moss. Nothing can form a softer couch, and when we think of ourselves as wearied in a pedestrian excursion, we fancy that a moss-covered bank, beneath an umbrageous tree, might be the luxury then most desirable. *(1869)*

Moss: recluse; ennui {boredom}

Moss rose: love; voluptuousness

Mouse-ear (scorpion grass, forget-me-not): "Forget me not"

Moving plant: agitation

Mugwort: happiness; travel; "Be not weary"

Mulberry tree: wisdom; "I will not survive you"

Mushroom: suspicion

Musk rose: capricious beauty

Myrobalan: bereavement

Myrrh (sweet cicely): gladness

MYRTLE, *Myrtus*: **LOVE.** The oak has ever been consecrated to Jupiter, the laurel to Apollo, the olive to Minerva, and the myrtle to Venus. Among the ancients the myrtle was a great favourite, for its elegance, and its sweet and glossy evergreen foliage. Its perfumed and delicate flowers seem destined to adorn the fair forehead of love, and are said to have been made the emblem of love, and dedicated to beauty, when Venus first sprang from the sea. We are informed by mythological writers that when the fair goddess first appeared upon the waves, she was preceded by the houris {a beautiful and voluptuous woman} with a scarf of a thousand colours, and a garland of myrtle. *(1839)*

Myrtle: love, positive; love in absence; passion, "Be my love"; peace; home; restfulness

Myrtle berry: treason

N

NARCISSUS, *Narcissus poeticus*: EGOTISM. The poet's narcissus exhales a very agreeable perfume; it bears a golden crown in the centre of its pure white petals, which expand quite flat, the stem slightly inclining to one side. The cup or nectary in the centre, which is very short, is frequently bordered with a bright purple circle, and sometimes the nectary is edged with crimson.

Ovid, in his Metamorphoses, tells us of the fate of the lovely and coy Narcissus. A thousand nymphs loved the handsome youth, but suffered the pains of unrequited love. Viewing himself in the crystal fount, he became enamoured of his own image. *(1839)*

Narcissus (poet's narcissus): self love; selfishness

Nasturtium (Indian cress): a war-like trophy; patriotism

Nasturtium, scarlet: splendor

Nettle, stinging: slander; cruelty

Night-blooming cereus: transient beauty

Night-smelling geranium: melancholy spirit

Nightshade (henbane, stinking nightshade): skepticism; dark thoughts; truth

Nosegay: gallantry

Nutmeg: "Your love is addicting"

O

Oak: hospitality; liberty

Oak leaf: bravery; bravery and humanity

Oats (quaking oats): music; the witching soul of music, hers

Oleander: Beware!

Olive tree: peace

**NARCISSUS POETICA, NASTURTIUM,
NIGHTSHADE, OAK LEAF.**

OATS, OLEANDER,
OLIVE, ORANGE BLOSSOM.

The Rose — The Myrtle — The Ivy

White Violet __ Small Bindweed __ Red & White Rosebud
Asiatic Ranunculus

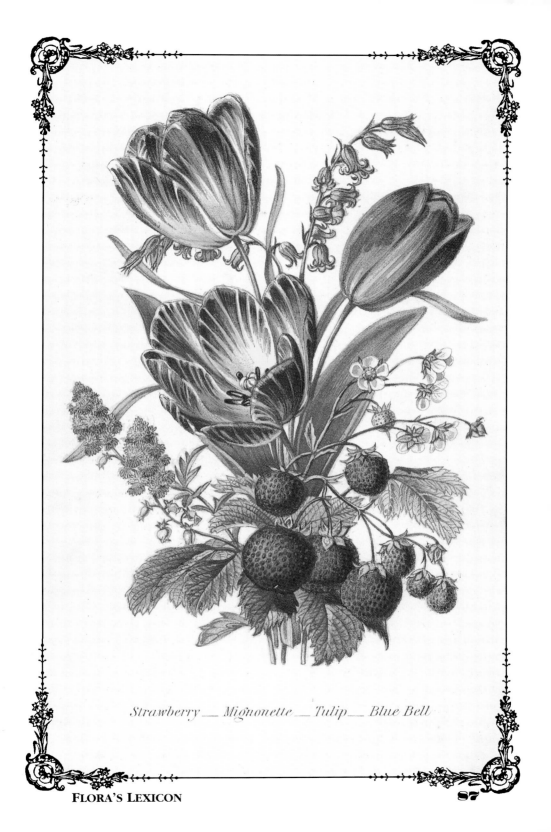

Strawberry __ Mignonette __ Tulip __ Blue Bell

Columbine ___ *Marigold* ___ *Pheasant's Eye*

Forget-me-not —— Hawthorn —— Lily of the Valley

Scarlet Ipomœa __ Honeysuckle __ White Heath __ Sweet Sultan.

Lilac,(purple & white) __ Marvel of Peru __ Spiderwort.

Pompon Rose___Star of Bethlehem___Primrose___Wood Sorrel.

ORANGE FLOWERS, *Citrus aurantium*: CHASTITY. The fair brow of a virgin bride is wreathed with a garland of Orange blossom, meet emblem of her maiden purity. This decoration is withheld from all who are undeserving of the distinction, more especially in the neighbourhood of Paris. *(1869)*

Orange blossom: "Your purity equals your loveliness"; woman's worth; bridal festivities

ORANGE TREE: GENEROSITY. This is a very handsome shrub, of a shining green through-out all seasons, never bare of most odoriferous flowers, and at all times bearing some of its brilliant, fragrant, and delicious fruit. It is the emblem of a generous friend whose countenance is ever radiant with good nature, whose lips cheer us with kindly words, and whose hands are ever open to bestow upon us his favours. *(1869)*

ORCHID, *Orchis*: A BELLE. A genus of near 90 species, principally indigenous to Europe, Northern Africa, and North America. Flowers orange, yellow, white, and bluish purple; spiked. *(1833)*

Oregano (wild marjoram): joy, happiness; joy on the mountain; "Add spice to your life!"*

Osier: frankness

Osmunda: dreams

Ox-eye (yellow oxeye daisy): patience; obstacle

Sentiment for Orchis: A Belle

Men gaze on beauty for a while,
  Allured by artificial smile;
  But Love shall never twang his dart
  From any string that's formed by art.

Paulding in *Flora's Interpreter,* 1833

P

Palm: victory

PANSY, *Viola tricolor*: **THINK OF ME.** Miss Twamley asks,

"Oh! are not Pansies emblems meet for thoughts?
The pure, the chequered: gay and deep by turns;
A hue for every mood the bright things wear
In their soft velvet coats."

and, as its English name seems to be a corruption of a French word in the phrase, *pensez-a-moi*: think of me, it is also called Heart's-ease, a sure result of a confident assurance that those whom we love are not unmindful of us when present or absent; not so unmindful, that is, to be careless and thoughtless of those claims we have upon their regard and affection. *(1869)*

Pansy: tender and pleasant thoughts; thoughts; love; "You occupy my thoughts"

Pray you, love, remember
There's Pansies: that's for thought.

Shakespeare in
Flora's Interpreter, 1833

Parsley: useful knowledge; feast, banquet; festivity; joy; victory; "The woman of the house is boss"

Pasque-flower anemone: "You are without pretension"

Passion flower: susceptibility; passionate love; religious superstition; Christian faith

Patience dock: patience

Pea, everlasting (perennial pea): an appointed meeting; "Wilt thou go with me?"

Pea, sweet: departure

Peach: "Your qualities like your charms are unequaled"

Peach blossom: "I am your captive"

Pear: affection

Pennyroyal: Flee away!; escape

Peony: anger, a frown; shy, bashful; bashful shame

Pepper: "Send me an answer"

PHLOX, BLACK SPRUCE PINE,
PITCH PINE, WHITE PERIWINKLE.

Pepper plant: satire

PEPPERMINT: **WARMTH OF SENTIMENT.** Menthes was surprised by Proserpine in the arms of her husband. The enraged goddess metamorphosed her rival into a plant, that appears to contain, in its double smell, the coldness of fear, and the ardour of love. We cultivate this plant under the name of peppermint, and we owe to it the drops that bear its name. *(1835)*

Peppermint: cordiality; wisdom
Periwinkle, blue: pleasures of memory
Periwinkle, white: pleasing reminiscences; early and sincere friendship; sweet recollections
Periwinkle, Madagascar: pleasures of memory
Persicaria: restoration
Persimmon: "Bury me amidst nature's beauty"
Petunia: "Do not despair"
Pheasant's eye (Adonis): sorrowful remembrances
Phlox: unanimity; unanimous, "We think alike"

PIMPERNEL, *Anagallis arvensis*: **ASSIGNATION.** The common pimpernel is a beautiful trailing weed opening its flowers regularly about eight minutes past seven o'clock, and closing them about three minutes past two o'clock. It serves, also, as an hygrometer; for, if rain fall, or there be much moisture in the atmosphere, the flowers either do not open, or close up again. It is frequently called the shepherd's weather-glass. *(1839)*

Pimpernel: change; the weather-glass
Pine: warm friendship; pity

"I'll go and peep at the Pimpernel,
 And see if she think the clouds look well;
For if the sun shine,
 And 'tis like to be fine,
I shall go to the fair,
 For my sweetheart is there:
So, Pimpernel, what bode the clouds
 and the sky?
 If fair weather, no maiden so merry as I."

Now the Pimpernel-flower had folded up
 Her little gold star in her coral cup,
And unto the maid
 Thus her warning said:
"Though the sun smile down,
 There's a gathering frown
O'er the chequer'd blue of the clouded sky;
 So tarry at home, for a storm is nigh."

Twamley in *Flora's Lexicon*, 1839

Pine, Black spruce fir: pity

Pine, pitch: time and philosophy

Pine, spruce: "Farewell!"

Pine tree: boldness; daring

PINEAPPLE, *Bromelia ananas*: YOU ARE PERFECT. The fruit of the pine apple, surrounded by its beautiful leaves, and surmounted by a crown in which the germ of a plant is concealed, seems as though it were sculptured in massy gold. It is so beautiful that it appears to be made to please the eyes; so delicious that it unites the various flavours of our best fruits; and so odoriferous that we should cultivate it if it were only for its perfume. *(1839)*

Pineapple: welcome

PINK, *Dianthus*: LIVELY AND PURE AFFECTION. Cultivation has doubled the petals of this favourite flower, and procured for it an infinite variety of colouring, so that it is painted with a thousand shades, from the delicate rose-colour to the perfect white; and from a deep red to a brilliant scarlet. In some varieties we observe opposite colours placed together on the same flower; the pure white is tipped with crimson, and the rose-coloured is streaked with lively and brilliant red. We also see these beautiful flowers marbled, speckled, and at other times bisected in such a manner that the deceived eye leads us to imagine that the same cup contains a purple flower, and one of the palest alabaster. *(1839)*

Pink: fascination

Pink, carnation: woman's love

Pink, China (Indian single, Indian pink): aversion; "You will always be lovely"

Pink, double: always lovely

Pink, pink (mountain pink): aspiring

Pink, red, double: pure and ardent love; woman's love

Pink, single: pure love

Pink, variegated: refusal

Pink, white: ingenuousness; "You are fair and fascinating"; talent

Plane tree: genius

Pleurisy root (swallow wort): cure for the heartache

Plum tree: "Retain your promises"; independence; keep your promise

Polyanthus (crimson heart): the heart's mystery

Polyanthus, lilac-colored (primula, primrose): confidence; pride of newly acquired fortune

Pomegranate: foolishness; foppishness

Pomegranate flower: mature and finished elegance

Pompom rose: loveliness

Poplar, white: time

Poplar, black: courage

POPPY, *Papaver*: **CONSOLATION OF SLEEP.** The poppy yields a narcotic juice in considerable quantity, which is frequently administered to procure sleep and relieve pain; on this account it has been made the symbol of consolation. The ancients, who regarded sleep as the great physician, and the great consoler of human nature, crowned the god of sleep with a wreath of poppies. *(1839)*

Poppy, red: consolation; evanescent {tending to vanish like a vapor} pleasure

Poppy, scarlet (wild poppy, field poppy): fantastic extravagance

Poppy, white: My Bane! My antidote!; forgetfulness, or consolation; sleep of the heart

Potato: beneficence {a charitable donation}

Potentilla: beloved daughter; "I claim, at least, your esteem"

Prickly pear (cactus): satire

Pride of China: dissension

PRIMROSE, *Primula*: **EARLY YOUTH.** The saffron tufts of the primrose announce the return of spring, when we see the snowy mantle of retiring winter ornamented with embroidery of verdure and of flowers. The season of hoar frost has passed, but the bright days of summer have not yet arrived. The period is emblematical of a lovely girl just passing from childhood to youth. *(1839)*

Primrose: "Have confidence in me"; a young girl passing from childhood to youth

Primrose, crimson heart: the heart's misery

Primrose, evening: inconstancy

Primrose, lilac-colored: confidence

Primrose, rose-colored: unpatronized merit

Primrose, scarlet: pride

Privet: mildness; prohibition; "It is forbidden"

Pulsatilla (pasque flower): "You have no claims"

PUMPKIN: **BULKINESS.** The pumpkin is usually large, and of considerable weight. It is sometimes said of a very stout person, that he resembles a Pumpkin. The comparison is vulgar, and cannot fail to be taken as an affront. *(1869)*

Pussy willow: symbol of Easter

Pyrus japonica: the fairie's fire

Quaking oats (oats): music; the witching soul of music, hers

QUAMOCLIT (American jasmine), *Ipomoea*: **BUSYBODY.** The name Quamoclit is an Indian one, used by the botanists Plumier and Tournefort as generic, but by Linnaeus only as a specific name of a pretty species of Ipomoea, sometimes called "busybody". It is a native of the East Indies. *(1839)*

Queen's rocket (dame's rocket, dame's violet): "You are the queen of coquettes"; "She will be fashionable"; fashion

QUINCE: TEMPTATION. The quince has been much celebrated in ancient poets; Virgil mentions, it is said, that the golden fruits in the garden of Hesperides were quinces, and it was these which tempted Hercules to attack the dragon that guarded them; in corroboration it is asserted that a statue of the demi-god is to be seen holding this fruit in his hand, as a trophy. It was likewise by means of golden quinces given him by Venus, that Hipponenes amused Atalanta during the race, and thus won her. It is also supposed that the fruit of the forbidden tree, that Eve, in an evil hour, was tempted to gather, was a quince, and not an apple, as is generally imagined. *(1835)*

R

Ragged robin (cuckoo flower): wit; dandy

Latin (frog)

RANUNCULUS, ASIATIC, *Ranunculus asiaticus*: **YOU ARE RADIANT WITH CHARMS.** The Asiatic ranunculus blooms amid our parterres in the earliest days of spring, spreading forth its varied lustrous flowers, which, shining with innumerable hues, are radiant with attractions. No other plant offers so rich a variety of colour to amateurs, "from a black down to white, through all the shades of reds, yellows, browns, and, indeed, excepting blue, every colour may be found in these gaily-painted flowers." *(1839)*

Ranunculus: "I am dazzled by your charms"

Raspberry: regrets; remorse; "I apologize"

Red bay: love's memory

Red mulberry: wisdom

Red valerian: readiness

REEDS: MUSIC.
> "the mingling sounds that come,
> Of shepherd's ancient reed."
>   Moore

Pan, who was devotedly fond of the fair Syrinx, pursued her one day upon the banks of the river Ladon, in Arcadia. The nymph entreated the river to help her, and when she was received into the stream, became transformed into Reeds. Pan cut several of the Reeds, of different sizes, and formed of them, as we are told, the first shepherd's pipe. Moore tells us that this is still a pastoral instrument of music in Syria. *(1869)*

Rest harrow {a weed}: obstacle.

Rhododendron (rose bay): ambition; danger, beware

Rock rose: safety

Rocket: rivalry

ROSE: BEAUTY. Who, that has ever been endowed with the power of song, has not sung of the Rose? Poets have not been able to exaggerate her beauty, nor to sing her praises to perfection. They have spoken of her, and with justice, as the daughter of the sky, the ornament of the earth, and the glory of Spring; but what words have ever expressed the charms of this lovely flower, her exquisite beauty, her matchless grace? When she spreads open her petals, the eye follows her harmonious outlines with delight. But how can we describe the rounded sections which form her entirety, the lovely tints so delicately laid upon her, the sweet perfume which she sends forth? Behold her, in the Spring, raising herself softly amid her elegant foliage, surrounded by her many buds; one might say that the Queen of flowers sports with the air which plays around her, that she adorns herself with diamond-like drops of dew which bathe her, that she smiles at the sun's rays which persuade her to display her charms. Nature seems to have exhausted her resources, in order to lavish upon her to excess, freshness, beauty of form, perfume, splendour, and loveliness. The Rose decorates the whole earth; she is one of the most common flowers.

On the day that the beauty of the Rose is perfected, it begins to fade; but each succeeding Spring restores her to us fresh and new. Poets have sung of her charms in vain; they have not made her praises grow old or become wearisome; and her name of itself keeps their productions fresh and attractive. The emblem of every age; the interpreter of all our sentiments; the Rose is mixed up with our festivals, with our joys and our sorrows. Innocent mirth crowns herself with Roses; simple modesty borrows her blushing tints; and we bestow a wreath of Roses as the reward of virtue. The

ROSES—MOSS FULL BLOWN, MOSS BUD,
MULTIFLORA, MUSK, CLUSTER, AND GLORIA MUNDI.

Rose is the image of youth, innocence, and harmless pleasure. She belongs to Venus, and even is the rival of her beauty; the Rose possesses, like her, charms more lovely than beauty. *(1869)*

Rose: love; genteel; pretty

ROSE MEANINGS BY COLOR

Rose meanings can be translated by color as well as by historic rose type. The author has updated rose meanings using antiquarian sources relating flowers and colors.

Coral: glory; "I admire your accomplishments"

Lavender: pure love; "My love is genuine"

Pink: grace; "You are gentle, graceful, lovely"

Red: love; desire; "I love you"

Red and white: warmth of heart; "May happiness be yours"

White: regard; "I am worthy of you"

Yellow: friendship; "I rejoice in your friendship"

ROSES AND THEIR MEANINGS

*From **Flora's Interpreter** by Sarah Josepha Hale, 1833*

ROSE, AUSTRIAN, *Rosa bicolor*: Thou art very lovely. A genus of nearly 50 species, chiefly indigenous to Europe. A few species found in Japan and India, and nine or ten in North America.

ROSE, BRIDAL, *Rubus rosafolius*: Happy love. Rose Bridal is of the genus Rubus, which includes the Bramble family. Flowers white, usually double, small and very beautiful.

ROSE, BURGUNDY, *Rosa parvifolia*: Simplicity and beauty. A dwarf shrub. Leaflet fine. Flowers small.

Resplendent rose! the flower of flowers,
Whose breath perfumes Olympus' bowers,
Whose virgin blush of chastened dye
Enchants so much our mental eye.

Greek poet in Tyas, 1869

ROSE, CAMPION (wild, briar rose), *Agrostemna githago*: Love's messengers. An European genus naturalized here: found in cornfields.

ROSE, CAROLINA, *Rosa carolina*: Love is dangerous. Shrubs six or seven feet high. Flowers crimson, large.

ROSE, CHINA, *Rosa multiflora*: Grace. Native of Japan and China. It is a shrub of luxuriant growth, flowers in clusters, said to be white in China, but here they are pink.

ROSE, CHINESE, DARK, *Rosa semperflorens*: Forsaken. Native of China, but naturalized in Europe. Leaflets of a dark shining green. Flowers solitary.

ROSE, DAMASK, *Rosa damascena*: Youth, freshness. The damask or damascena rose was first brought from Asia into Greece: then it was transplanted into Italy and France. Flowers white and red.

ROSE, DAMASK, *Rosa damascena*: Bashful love. Native of Syria and Damascus, though naturalized in Europe. It is deliciously sweet. Flowers a beautiful pink, verging towards a purple.

ROSE, DEEP-RED, *Rosa rubor*: Bashful shame. This is the wild sweet rose, improved by cultivation. It is the most common species in our gardens.

ROSE, HUNDRED-LEAVED, *Rosa centifolia*: Dignity of mind, pride. This magnificent rose is a native of the southern parts of Europe. The velvet rose belongs to this species. Its colors vary from crimson to pink and purple.

ROSE, MOSS, *Rosa muscosa*: Superior merit. Native of the south of Europe. Stem three or four feet high: flowers at the top of the branch large, very fragrant, of a bright crimson hue: flowers double.

ROSE BUD, MOSS, *Rosa muscosa*: Confession. A rose bud just opening, according to Berkley's Utopia, is a declaration of love.

ROSE, MULTIFLORA (bramble flowered Chinese rose): Grace.

ROSE, MUNDI, *Rosa versicolor*: You are merry. An American rose, being a variety of the species *lucida.* Found from New York to Carolina. Flowers elegantly striped or variegated with red and white.

ROSE, MUSK, *Rosa moschata*: Charming. The musk rose is exceedingly beautiful. Native of Barbary, and from its petals the essential oil is obtained, called "Otto of Roses."

ROSE BUD, RED, *Rosa rubrifolia*: May you ever be pure and lovely. There is no emblem more significant of youth, beauty, and innocence, than a rose-bud. The rubrifolia is a native of North America.

Be your heart as pure,
Your cheek as bright
As the spring rose.

Miss Loudon in
Flora's Interpreter,
1833

ROSE, RED-LEAVED, *Rosa rubrifolia*: Beauty and prosperity. Native of Switzerland and Savoy. Stem erect. The whole plant, branches, leaves, stalks and the tube of the calyx are more or less tinged with red.

ROSE, THORNLESS, *Rosa inermis*: Ingratitude. Native of Switzerland and North America. The stem is five or six feet high, without a prickle: and Lemaistre asserts that the thorns on the other species have been produced by cultivation: hence the emblem, ingratitude. Flowers crimson.

ROSE, WHITE, *Rosa alba*: Sadness. The rose was sacred to Venus, and the fable says, was originally white, but the goddess being wounded by a thorn, the blood "On the white rose being shed, made it forever red."

ROSE, WHITE, WITHERED, *Rosa alba*: I am in despair. Native of Europe. The bush is five or six feet high. Leaves dark green. Flowers usually pure white, but sometimes tinged with a delicate blush.

ROSE, YELLOW, *Rosa lutea*: Let us forget. The yellow rose is a native of Italy. They are both single and double, and have the odor of a pine-apple.

ROSE, YORK AND LANCASTER, *Rosa versicola*: War. This species was the common dog-rose: the red adopted by the house of Lancaster, the white by that of York.

Oh! I love the sweet blooming, the pretty moss rose,
  'Tis the type of true pleasure, and perfected joy;
Oh! I envy each insect that dares to repose
  'Midst its leaves, or among its soft beauties to toy.

I love the sweet lily, so pure and so pale,
  With a bosom as fair as the new-fallen snows;
Her luxuriant odours she spreads through the vale,
  Yet e'en she must yield to my pretty moss rose.

Oh! I love the gay hearts-ease, and violet blue,
  The sun-flower and blue-bell, each flow'ret that blows,
The fir-tree, the pine-tree, acacia, and yew,
  Yet e'en these must yield to my pretty moss rose.

Yes, I love my moss rose, for it ne'er had a thorn,
  'Tis the type of life's pleasures, unmix'd with its woes;
'Tis more gay, and more bright, than the opening morn:
  Yes, all things must yield to my pretty moss rose.

Anonymous in *Flora's Lexicon*, 1839

Rose acacia: elegance

Rose, cabbage: the ambassador of love

Rose, daily: "That smile I would aspire to!"

Rose, dried: death preferable to loss of innocence

Rose, full blown: "You are beautiful"

ROSE IN A TUFT OF GRASS: THERE IS EVERY THING TO BE GAINED BY GOOD COMPANY. The poet Sadi said, "One day I saw a rose-bush surrounded by a tuft of grass. What! I cried, does that vile plant dare to place itself in the company of Roses? I was about to tear the grass away, when it meekly addressed me, saying, 'Spare me! I am not the Rose, it is true; but, from my perfume, any one may know at least that I have lived with Roses.' " How anxiously should we seek the company of those whose intellectual and moral character surpasses our own, that we may drink in some of their mind's wealth and moral worth, and so far be improved by the association. *(1869)*

Rose leaf: "I am never importunate"

Rose, maiden's blush: "If you do love me, you will find me out"

I do betray myself with blushing!
Shakespeare

ROSE, MOSS, *Rosa muscosa*: PLEASURE WITHOUT ALLOY. The elegant moss rose is commonly supposed to be the offspring of the Provence rose, though some consider it to belong to the family of hundred-leaved roses. It has ever been made the emblem of perfected joy; Milton mentions it as "without thorn, the rose"; and an anonymous writer has sung of it in that character. *(1839)*

Rose, unique: "Call me not beautiful"

Rose, white, withered: transient impressions

Rose, without a thorn: ingratitude

Rose, yellow: the decrease of love on better aquaintance

Rose-scented geranium: preference

Rosebud: youth; beauty; innocence; young girl

Rosebud, red: "You are young and beautiful"; "May you ever be pure and lovely"

Rosebud, white: a heart that is ignorant of love; too young to love; "The heart that knows not love"

Rosehips: the fruits of love

ROSEMARY: **YOUR PRESENCE REVIVES ME.** This shrub yields by distillation a light pale essential oil of great fragrance, which is imparted to rectified spirit. It was formerly recommended for strengthening the nervous system, headaches, etc., as well as to strengthen the memory. Rosemary has also been made the emblem of fidelity, and used accordingly, to be worn at weddings, and, on the same principle, at funerals. It is the principal ingredient in Hungary water, and is drunk at tea for headaches, and by nervous persons. *(1839)*

Reverend sirs,
For you there's rosemary and rue; these keep
Seeming and savour all the winter long:
Grace and remembrance be to you both.

Shakespeare in *Flora's Lexicon*, 1839

Rosemary: remembrance; loyalty, fidelity

Rudbeckia: justice

RUE, *Ruta graveolens*: **GRACE OR PURIFICATION.** This plant was formerly called Herb of Grace, from its being used to sprinkle holy water.

"Here did she drop a tear; here in this place
I'll set a bank of rue, sour herb of grace."

Rue: disdain; grief; clear vision; manners or morals; herb of grace and understanding; virtue; repentance

Rush: docility

SAGE, DARK PURPLE SCARIUS, SCARLET
LYCHNIS, SIBERIAN CRAB TREE, SNAP DRAGON.

SAFFRON, *Crocus sativus*: **DO NOT DECEIVE YOURSELVES.** A light infusion of Saffron tends to raise the spirits; but if indulged in to excess it produces intoxication. If its emanations be inhaled in moderation, it is said to be restorative; if too freely breathed, the effect is injurious. *(1869)*

Saffron crocus: marriage; joy, laughter

Saffron flower: "Do not abuse"; "Excess is dangerous"

SAGE: **ESTEEM.** This plant derives its scientific name from *salvere,* to save, from its supposed powers of healing. The genus, which is very large, consists of herbs whose leaves are generally of a rugose appearance, and of a very aromatic smell. In debility of the stomach it is used as a tonic by the Chinese, who consider that it has the effect of strengthening the nervous system; and it is said for these purposes they prefer it to their own tea. *(1840)*

Sage: domestic virtues; long life and good health; "I will suffer all for you"

Saint John's Wort: superstition; animosity

Salvia, blue: "I think of you"

Salvia, red: energy

Santolina: protection; ward off evil

Savory: interest; spiciness; "The truth may be bitter"

Scabiosa (mourning bride, sweet scabious): unfortunate attachment; "I have lost all"

Scarlet geranium: consolation; stupidity

Scarlet lychnis: sunbeamed eyes

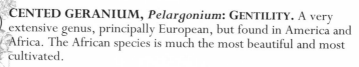

SCENTED GERANIUM, *Pelargonium*: GENTILITY. A very extensive genus, principally European, but found in America and Africa. The African species is much the most beautiful and most cultivated.

> And genteel geranium
>   With a leaf for all who come.

>   —Hunt

The characteristic of true gentility is the talent to discern the feelings of those around us, and the tact to please each one by appropriate attentions. As the Geranium offers so large a variety of species to gratify every taste, it is appropriately called genteel. I shall give the interpretations which have been affixed to a few of the species: the authority by which these have been bestowed, must be in the general application of the one quoted above. *(1833)*

Scented geranium, apple: present preference

Scented geranium, grey or silver leaf: recall

Scented geranium, lemon: tranquility of mind; unexpected meeting

Scented geranium, nutmeg: an expected meeting

Scented geranium, oak leaf: "Lady, deign to smile"; true friendship

Scented geranium, peppermint: cordial feelings*

Scented geranium, rose: preference

Scotch fir: elevation

SEA THRIFT, *Statice maritima*: SYMPATHY. The generic name of this plant is Greek, and denotes that which has the property of fixing, uniting, and retaining. The flowers are small, very numerous, turning towards the sky, forming pretty purple blue spikes. They are very ornamental border flowers, but require considerable care. Naturally the plants prefer marshy places, and especially the shores of the sea, where they seem to bind the sands together by their abundant roots. *(1869)*

Sensitive plant (mimosa): sensitiveness; bashful modesty

> Weak with nice sense the chast Mimosa stands,
>   And from each touch withdraws her timid hands;
>   Oft as light clouds o'erpass the summer glade,
>   Alarmed she trembles at the moving shade.

>   Darwin in *Flora's Interpreter*, 1833

Serpentine cactus: horror

Service tree: prudence

Shaking saintfoin: agitation

Small bindweed (wild morning glory): humility

Snapdragon: presumption and desperation

Snowball (Guelder rose): to bind; thoughts of heaven; good news

SNOWDROP, *Galanthus*: CONSOLATION. "The north wind whistles, and the hoar frost clothes the verdure-despoiled trees; an uniform white carpet covers the earth, the birds withhold their tuneful song, and the sealed waters cease to murmur as they roll along; the rays of the sun, unfeebled by the density of our atmosphere, shed a gloomy light over our fields; and the heart of man is sad, while all nature reposes in torpid tranquillity."

Thus Madame de La Tour describes the state of nature, when suddenly a delicate flower pierces through the veil of snow which had concealed it. It has been aptly termed by her countrymen *Perce neige,* from the quality just named; and is with equal propriety called snow-drop in America. *(1839)*

Snowdrop: refinement; friendship in adversity; adventurous friendship

Sorrel (wild sorrel, oxalis): wit ill-timed; parental affection

Southernwood: perseverance; constancy; dreams of a lover; jest or bantering

Spearmint: warmth of sentiment; friendliness

Speedwell (veronica): female fidelity

Spider orhrys: skill

Spiderwort: "I esteem, but do not love you"; transient happiness

Spindle tree (euonymus): "Your charms are traced upon my heart"

Spiroea (meadowsweet): uselessness

Spotted arum (lords and ladies): warmth

Spruce, black: pity

Spruce, Norway: hope in adversity

Spruce, pine: farewell

Spurge laurel (daphne): coquetry; desire to please

SQUIRTING CUCUMBER, *Momordica elaterium*: CRITICISM.
Adverse criticism produces a painful effect upon the unfortunate object of it, therefore the specific name of this plant has suggested it as the proper symbol of the biting operation. *(1869)*

STAR OF BETHLEHEM, *Ornithogalum umbellatum*: PURITY.
The "Bright-eyed Star of Bethlehem" is indigenous, but it is a welcome plant in our gardens. From April to June it bears an umbel of star-like flowers, white as the purest milk. There is no dweller in our borders more agreeable in its whole appearance than it, and none more pure and pleasing. *(1869)*

Star of Bethlehem (summer snowflake): reconciliation; "the light of our path"

Starwort: afterthought; welcome to a stranger

Stephanotis: "Will you accompany me to the East?"

Straw, whole: union; contract

Straw, broken: broken contract

Strawberry: perfection; foresight; perfect goodness; "You are perfect"

Strawberry tree: esteem and love

Strawflower: always remembered

Succory (chicory): frugality

Sumac (smokebush): splendor; intellectual excellence

Sunflower: false riches

Sunflower, dwarf: your devout ardorer

Sunflower, tall (common sunflower): pride, haughtiness; lofty and pure thoughts

Swallow-wort (celandine, pleurisy root): cure for the heartache; medicine

SWEET BAY, *Laurus nobilis*: **TREACHERY.** It was formerly a common practice in making custards, to throw into the pan a few leaves of Laurel, in order to flavour them. Where the party preparing them was well acquainted with properties of the leaves, care was taken to limit the quantity so as to produce an agreeable flavour; but if too many were used they always produced a deleterious effect, and not seldom death has ensued where the quantity has been in excess; hence the tree has been made emblematic of Treachery. *(1869)*

Sweet briar: simplicity

Sweet cicely: gladness

Sweet flag: fitness

SWEET PEA, *Lathyrus odoratus*: **DEPARTURE.** The sweet pea is a native of Ceylon and of Sicily. Its fragrance is thought to resemble a mixture of the orange-flower and the rose. It richly merits the appellation of sweet. The form of the flower is peculiarly graceful.

Sweet pea: delicate pleasure

Sweet rocket (dame's rocket): deceit

Sweet-scented coltsfoot: "We will do you justice"

Sweet sultan (centaury): felicity {great happiness, bliss}

SWEET WILLIAM, *Dianthus barbatus*: **CHILDHOOD.** This is a species of pink, a native of Germany. It is much cultivated in our rural gardens, and on account of the brilliancy of its flowers and its agreeable fragrance is deservedly a great favourite with children. The firmness and solidity of its bunches of flowers make it a safe plaything for them. *(1839)*

Put by thy work, dear mother;
Dear mother come with me,
For I've found within the garden,
The beautiful sweet-pea!

And bending on their stalks, mother,
Are roses white and red;
And pale-stemm'd balsams all a-blow,
On every garden-bed.

Put by thy work, I pray thee,
And come out, mother dear!
We used to buy these flowers,
But they are growing here!

Oh, mother! little Amy,
Would have loved these flowers to see;
Dost remember how we tried to get
For her a pink sweet-pea!

Dost remember how she loved
Those rose-leaves pale and sere?
I wish she had but lived to see
The lovely roses here!

Put by thy work, dear mother,
And wipe those tears away!
And come into the garden
Before 'tis set of day!

Flora's Lexicon, 1839

Sweet William: finesse; a smile; craftiness; gallantry

Sycamore: curiosity; woodland beauty; reserve

SYRINGA **(mock orange),** *Philadelphus*: MEMORY. This fragrant flower is made the emblem of memory, because when once we inhale its penetrating odour, it continues to dwell on the sense for a considerable time. *(1839)*

Syringa (mock orange): disappointment

Syringa, Carolina: disappointment

Tamarisk: crime

TANSY, *Tanacetum*: RESISTANCE. This balsamic plant, so celebrated of old, is made the emblem of resistance, because it was supposed to act against contagion. *(1839)*

> *Before my door the box-edged border lies,*
> *Where flowers of mint, and thyme, and tansy rise.*
> Scott in *Flora's Lexicon*

Tansy: life everlasting, immortality; hostile thoughts

Tansy, wild: "I declare war against you"

Tarragon: unselfish sharing; lasting interest

TEASEL, *Dipsacus fullonum*: MISANTHROPY. It is not easy to perceive why this should be the emblem of Misanthropy. It is a prickly plant, and requires two years from the time of being sown to grow to full ripeness. The prickly awns with which they are beset make the Teasel most useful, as being the best means known whereby clothiers are able to raise the nap upon our beautiful broadcloth. *(1869)*

Ten-week stock: promptitude

THORN APPLE, THYME, TIGER FLOWER,
TRUMPET FLOWER, TUBEROSE.

Thistle: misanthropy; austerity; sternness

Thorn apple: deceitful charms; "I dreamed of thee"

Thrift: sympathy

THYME, *Thymus serpyllum*: **ACTIVITY.** The Greeks regarded Thyme as the emblem of Activity. No doubt they observed that its perfume, which stimulates the brain, is very wholesome to elderly people, whose energies it seems to restore.

Action is characteristic of the soldier, and is always allied with true courage; wherefore, in the days gone by, ladies were often wont to embroider the scarf for their knights with the figure of a bee humming around a sprig of Thyme. This two-fold symbol implied, moreover, that he who adopted it, was gentle in all his acts. *(1869)*

Thyme: thriftiness; happiness; courage

Thyme, lemon: enjoyable activity; "My time with you is a pleasure"*

Thyme, nutmeg: sincere devotion*

Thyme, silver-leaf: "Remember our happiness"*

Tiger flower: "For once may pride befriend me"

Toothwort: concealment

Trefoil (purple clover): providence

Trembling poplar: moaning

Tremella: resistance, opposition

Trumpet flower, ash-leaved: separation

Tuberose: a sweet voice; voluptuousness

TULIP (red), *Tulipa sylvestris*: **DECLARATION OF LOVE.** On the banks of the Bosphorus, the Tulip represents Inconstancy; but it also is the emblem of the most violent love. Those which grow naturally in the fields of Byzantium, with petals of fiery red and centres black as though burnt, say to a captive beauty, that one loves her, and, if she will show herself to him for a moment, her appearance will make his countenance as of fire, and his heart like coal. Thus a young man fresh or green from the hands of nature, yields an homage without disguise; but when fashioned by the world, as the tulip is manipulated by the hands of the gardener, he becomes more amiable, more lovely, but he has ceased to love.

The tulip is so called from its shape resembling that of the turban. Its emblematic power, if it does not sufficiently express a declaration of love, may well speak of that mania which exceeded the madness of the most ardent love in times past; for under its influence men did the most insane things. *(1869)*

Tulip, red: admiration
Tulip, variegated: beautiful eyes
Tulip, yellow: hopeless love
Tulip tree blossom: rural happiness; fame; happiness
Turnip: charity
Tussilage, sweet-scented: "You shall have justice"

Valerian: an accommodating disposition
Vanilla: sweetness
Venus fly-trap: deceit

VENUS'S LOOKING-GLASS, *Campanula speculum*: **FLATTERY.** This is a pretty annual border-flower of great beauty, which, from May to August, opens its shining purple flowers in our fields so soon as the sun sheds his golden light upon them. If clouds should intercept his rays, then the sensitive petals close themselves as at the approach of night. A fanciful fable tells us that Venus let one of her mirrors fall upon the earth. A shepherd found this bijou, and looking upon it, as it had the power of reflecting an image more beautiful than the reality, he forgot his mistress, and cared for nothing but to admire himself in the glass. Cupid, fearing the consequences of so great an error, broke the glass and transformed the pieces into this pretty Campanula, which has ever since borne the name of Venus's Looking-glass. *(1869)*

Verbena (vervain): sensibility; enchantment; superstition
Verbena, pink: family union
Verbena, scarlet: unite against evil

**RED AND YELLOW TULIP, TULIP TREE BLOSSOM,
VENUS'S LOOKING GLASS, VERBENA OR VERVAIN.**

Verbena, white: "Pray for me"

Veronica (speedwell): female fidelity; fidelity

Vernal grass {a sweet-scented grass}: "We may be poor, but we will be happy"

Vervain (verbena): sensibility; enchantment; superstition

Viburnum (Laurustinus): a token

Viburnum, snowball: thoughts of heaven

Vine: intoxication

VIOLET, *Viola*: MODESTY. Ion, the Greek name of this flower, is traced by some etymologists to Ia, the daughter of Midas, who was betrothed to Atys, and changed by Diana into a violet, to hide her from Apollo. The beautiful modest flower still retains the bashful timidity of the nymph, partially concealing itself amidst foliage from the garish gaze of the sun. Hence it has been ingeniously given as a device to an amiable and witty lady of a timid and reserved disposition, surrounded with the motto: "I must be sought after." *(1839)*

Violet is for faithfulness,
Which in me shall abide;
Hoping, likewise, that
from your heart
You will not let it slide.

Shakespeare's Sonnets
in *Flora's Lexicon*,
1839

Little need be said to increase the universal admiration of this favourite flower, for there is not one more sought after than it, nor does any yield us greater pleasure when found in the early Spring. We admire the embossed leaves, the drooping purple flower, and are enchanted with its delicious fragrance. Then, as we roam through rustic lanes, or by the hedgerow, or the border of a wood, how pleasant it is to find that,

> *"Where the banks are wet with drops of morning dew,*
> *The gentle Violet steals out, in hood of blue."*
> Taylor

The fondness of this flower for the most retired spots, over-grown by grass, often in the very depth of the hawthorn hedge, where its presence can only be detected by the fragrance which Zephyr steals from her in passing, and diffuses through space, has made the Sweet-scented Violet the proper emblem of Modesty; and so Miss Taylor sings of it.

Down in a green and shady bed, a modest Violet grew;
  Its stalk was bent, it hung its head, as if to hide from view.

And yet it was a lowly flower, its colour bright and fair;
  It might have graced a rosy bower, instead of hiding there.

Yet thus it was content to bloom, in modest tints arrayed;
  And there diffused a sweet perfume, within the silent shade.
                                                    Tyas, 1869

Violet, blue: love; faithfulness; sweetness; loyalty

Violet, white: modesty; innocence; candour

Violet, yellow: rural happiness

Virgin's bower (clematis): filial {relating to a son or daughter} love; mental beauty

ALLFLOWER, *Cherianthus fruticulosus*: **FAITHFUL IN ADVERSITY.** We find this fragrant flower blooming in places where ruin and desolation prevail. In the cracks of ancient walls, in nooks and corners of shattered towers, on cottages and tombs in decay, there we may find the wall-flower. In short, wherever adversity and misfortune have befallen masonry of old, valued for what it has been, there this flower flourishes, faithful to the friends who cherished it when they were prosperous and gay. *(1869)*

Wallflower: fidelity in misfortune

Walnut, black: intellect

Water lily, white (lotus flower): purity of heart; eloquence

Watermelon: bulkiness

Weeping willow: forsaken; forsaken lover; melancholy; mourning

Weigela: "Accept a faithful heart"

Wheat: prosperity; riches

Wisteria: "Welcome, fair stranger"

Witch hazel: a spell

Wood hyacinth (harebell, bluebell): delicacy; kindness; delicate and lonely as this flower

OOD SORREL, *Oxalis*: **JOY.** The wood sorrel, vulgarly called "cuckoo's bread", flowers very freely, about Easter. This pretty little plant shuts its leaves, closes its corollas, and the flowers hang pendent and drooping from the stems. They seem to yield themselves to sleep; but at the first dawn of day we may say that they are filled with joy, for they throw back their leaves, and expand their flowers; and we doubt not it is on this account that peasants have said that they sing the praises of the Creator. *(1839)*

Wood sorrel (oxalis, true shamrock): maternal tenderness

Woodbine (bush honeysuckle): fraternal love

Woodruff, sweet: modest worth; "Be cheerful and rejoice in life"

ORMWOOD: ABSENCE. La Fontaine says, "Absence is the worst of evils," and wormwood is the most bitter of plants; its name is derived from the Greek, it signifies Without Sweetness. *(1835)*

Wormwood: displeasure

REATH OF WHITE DAISIES: I WILL THINK OF IT. In the days of chivalry, when a lady, to speak in common parlance, "didn't know her own mind"; that is to say, was not determined either to accept or refuse the suit of her lover, she used to wear on her brow a Wreath of White Daisies, by which she wished to say to him, "I will think of it." *(1869)*

Y

YARROW, *Achillea millefolium*: **WAR.** Milfoil, or Yarrow, cicatrizes {forms scar tissue on} all wounds made by iron. It is said that Achilles, whose name it bears, used it to cure the wounds of Telephus. Its having received from the ancients the name of this celebrated hero renders it a very appropriate emblem of war. *(1839)*

Yarrow (achillea, milfoil): to cure; cure for heartache; health; foretelling the future

Yellow narcissus: disdain

YELLOW ROSE: **UNFAITHFULNESS.** Yellow is the colour which we usually assign to faults of unfaithfulness. The Yellow Rose seems the flower which properly represents those who are guilty of it. Water wearies it, the sun burns it. Constraint can alone bring this Rose, which has no fragrance, into good condition. It does not improve with care, nor yet when it enjoys freedom. When one would wish to see it at its best, we must bend its buds down to the earth, secure them in that position, and then it will flourish. *(1869)*

YEW TREE, *Taxus baccata*: **SADNESS.** The Yew-tree has always been considered the suitable ornament of churchyards, and so has become associated with sad recollections. It is not a favourite tree with us. Its appearance, when left to grow at will, is gloomy and heavy. We had occasion to plant trees in a churchyard, and we preferred the cheerful Lime-tree, which has grown and prospered, and added much to the light and airy aspect of the village cemetery. We were offered some Yew-trees, which we declined with thanks. Where our brothers and sisters sleep the sleep of death, there ought we to feel all the comfort that we can feel, in the hope that they enjoy a better life than this, and look forward, without dread or despondency, to the time when we shall be permitted to rejoin them.

Sir Walter Scott agrees with all other poets in regarding the Yew-tree as having a sad and gloomy appearance, and as producing a corresponding feeling in the mind. *(1869)*

The Yew, which, in the place of sculptured stone,
Marks out the resting-place of men unknown.

Churchill

Yew: penitence; sorrow

Yoke elm: ornament

ZINNIA, *Zinnia*: **ABSENCE.** This flower received its singular name from a German botanist, Dr. John G. Zinn. We have many species of this genus in America. The red is found on the banks of the Mississippi; the yellow is a native of Peru; the scarlet, the purple-flowered and slender-flowered, of Mexico. *(1839)*

Zinnia: thoughts of absent friends

The Zinnia's solitary flower,
Which blooms in forests lone and deep,
Are like the visions fair and bright,
That faithful, absent hearts will keep.

Anonymous in
Flora's Interpreter, 1833

Sweet pea, pansy
"I depart. Think on me."

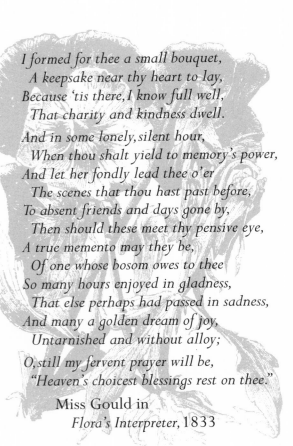

I formed for thee a small bouquet,
  A keepsake near thy heart to lay,
Because 'tis there, I know full well,
  That charity and kindness dwell.

And in some lonely, silent hour,
  When thou shalt yield to memory's power,
And let her fondly lead thee o'er
  The scenes that thou hast past before,
To absent friends and days gone by,
  Then should these meet thy pensive eye,
A true memento may they be,
  Of one whose bosom owes to thee
So many hours enjoyed in gladness,
  That else perhaps had passed in sadness,
And many a golden dream of joy,
  Untarnished and without alloy;

O, still my fervent prayer will be,
  "Heaven's choicest blessings rest on thee."

Miss Gould in
  Flora's Interpreter, 1833

FLORA'S SENTIMENTS

Tulip
"Declaration of love"

Rose   **_Violet_**
"Beauty"   _"Modesty"_

**_"Your beauty and modesty have forced
from me a declaration of love."_**

Notes: Meanings created by the author (see page xi) are indicated with an asterisk (*). Extended meanings in this section are taken from The Poetical Language of Flowers, or The Pilgrimage of Love *by Thomas Miller, London, 1847; artwork is reproduced from* Le Langage des Fleurs *by Emma Faucon, Paris (not dated).*

Abandon: Anemone

ABSENCE: **Wormwood.** Its derivation signifies, without sweetness; and so far may Absence be put down as the bitterness of Love.

Absence: Zinnia
Absurdity: Dandelion
Abuse, "Do not abuse": Saffron flower

ACCOMMODATING DISPOSITION: **Red valerian.** Will grow on old walls, ruins, or almost anywhere; hence its floral signification.

✓**Accomplishment**, "I admire your accomplishments": Coral rose

Accomplishment, "I overcome everything": Mistletoe

Acknowledgment: Campanula, Lavender

Activity: Thyme

Admiration: Heather, Tulip

Admiration, "I admire but cannot love you": Bay

Admiration, "I admire your accomplishments": Coral rose

Adore, "Your devout adorer": Dwarf sunflower

Adversity, energy in: Camomile

Adversity, love undiminished by: Dogwood

Affection: Cockscomb, Morning glory, Pear

✓**Affection**, beyond the grave: Locust tree

Affection, fraternal: Mock orange

Affection, generous and devoted: Honeysuckle

Affection, return of, "I desire a return of affection": Jonquil

Affection, return of, "I reciprocate your affection": Feverfew

Tulipes.
Qui vous connait vous admire. ADMIRATION

Tulips
ADMIRATION
He who knows
you, admires you

A FFECTIONATE REMEMBRANCE: **Rosemary.** "That's for Remembrance: I pray you, love, remember," says the sweet Ophelia. And who would wish to change the emblem of a flower which Shakespeare has made immortal?

Affections: Marigold

Affliction: Aloe

A FTERTHOUGHT: **Michaelmas daisy.** Which blows when the flowers of summer have faded: coming unaware, like a pleasant thought.

Afterthought: Starwort

Aging not: Ageratum

Agreement, "We think alike": Phlox

Ambition: Hollyhock, Rhododendron

Ambition, "The ambition in my love thus plagues itself": Fuchsia

Ambition, female: White hollyhock

A MIABILITY: **White jasmine.** Its sweetness, and beauty, and star-like flowers, bear about them a resemblance to an amiable lady. Gilbert White saw this in the drooping form of the silver-stemmed Birch, when he called it the "Lady of the Wood". He would have added "Amiable", had it been starred with beautiful flowers like the Jasmine.

Angel, "You are my angel": Cowslip

A NGER: **Gorse.** A pretty, though formidable plant, armed up to the very gold of the flowers, and piercing those who approach not its beauty carefully.

Anger: Peony

Animosity: Saint John's Wort

Annoyance, "Stop your pestering": Butterfly weed

Answer, "I would not answer hastily": Honeysuckle

Answer, "Send me an answer": Pepper

Anticipation: Anemone

Anxiety, "Please relieve my anxiety": Christmas rose

Anxious and trembling: Red columbine

Apology, "I apologize": Raspberry

Apology, "Let us make up": Lily of the valley

Appreciation: Flax

Architecture: Candytuft
Ardour: Cuckoo-pink, German iris
Argument: Fig
Arrogance: Scarlet lobelia
Artifice: Clematis

A RTS: **Acanthus.** Worthily placed in honour of Callimachus, who is said to have formed from its beauty the capital of the Corinthian column, as he saw it growing over the grave of a young maiden.

Aspiring: Pink

A SSIGNATION: **Pimpernel.** Its regularity in opening and shutting is well selected as denoting an appointment between lovers, who are supposed to trust more to the bright sunshine and sweet flowers, and the feelings of their own hearts, than the measured minutes of Time. It also denotes change in the weather, as the flowers always close before the rain. By country people it is called the Shepherd's Weatherglass.

Asylum: Juniper
Attachment, ardent: Larkspur
Attachment, devoted: Heliotrope
Attachment, "I attach myself to you": Jasmine
Attention: Begonia
Attention, constant personal: Lavender
Austerity: Thistle
Aversion: Pink

Pensées.
ATTACHEMENT
Le mien s'accroît chaque jour.

Pansies
ATTACHMENT
Mine grows every day

Bane, "My bane! My antidote!": Poppy
Banquet: Parsley
Bantering: Southernwood
Bashful: Peony

B ASHFULNESS: **Maiden's blush rose.** One of the most beautiful and delicate of all the queenly class of roses.

Bashful modesty: Sensitive plant

BEAUTY: **Rose.** Its very name is beautiful: and more than two thousand years ago it was worshipped by the poets, and called the Queen of Flowers.

Beauty: Carnation, Rosebud

Beauty, and innocence: English daisy

Beauty, and prosperity: Red-leaved rose

Beauty, capricious: Lady's slipper, Musk rose

Beauty, delicate: Hibiscus

Beauty, ever new: Damask rose, Monthly rose

Bouquet of Roses
BEAUTY
It is without equal

Beauty, in solitude: Heather

Beauty, lasting: Gillyflower

Beauty, of mind: Clematis

Beauty, pensive: Laburnum

Beauty, splendid: Amaryllis

Beauty, transient: Night blooming cereus

Beauty, unfading: Gillyflower

Beauty, unknown to the possessor: Red daisy

Beauty, woodland: Sycamore

Beauty, worth beyond beauty: Alyssum

Beauty, "You are beautiful, but timid": Amaryllis

BELIEF: **Passion flower.** Has become strangely woven with our faith, from a fancied resemblance to a cross and a crown, although it requires a great effort of the imagination to call up either the one or the other. Still its very name, in some measure, renders it sacred to Faith and Belief.

Belle: Orchid

Beneficence: Potato, Marsh mallow

Benevolence: Carolina allspice

Bereavement: Myrobalan

Best wishes: Sweet basil

Betray, "We are betrayed": Caraway

Beware: Oleander, Rhododendron

Bewitched, "You have bewitched me": Lemon verbena

Birth: Dittany

Birth, prolific: Fig tree

Birth, pride of: Crown imperial

Bitterness: Aloe

Bluntness: Borage

Blushes: Sweet marjoram

Boaster: Hydrangea

Boldness: Pine tree, Larch

Bonds: Morning glory

Bonds of affection: Gillyflower

Boss, "The woman of the house is boss": Parsley

Bravery: Oak leaf

Bridal favor: Ivy geranium

Bridal festivities: Orange blossom

Brusqueness: Borage

Bulkiness: Pumpkin, Watermelon

Burn, "I burn": Cactus, Red iris

Bury, "Bury me amidst nature's beauty": Persimmon

Busybody: Quamoclit

Calmness: Buckbean

Calumny {a misrepresentation intended to blacken another's reputation}: Christmas rose, Madder

CANDOUR: **White violet.** The wood spirits looked into some of the Violets until they partook of the hue of their own deep-blue eyes; and others, which were before of a dark purple, they buried in their own snowy bosoms, until they faded into a pearly white, then laughingly planted them again in the ground, causing them for ever to partake of the candour, and sweetness, and innocence of the tender hearts on which they were first nursed, and the gentle spirit by whose purity their colour was changed.

Captive, "I am your captive": Peach blossom

Captivation: Field convolvulus

Chagrin: Marigold

Chance, by chance: Locust tree

Change: Pimpernel

Change, likely to change frequently without reason: Wild honeysuckle

Change, natural: Locust tree
Charity: Wild grape, Turnip
Charm against evil: Garlic
Charming: Musk rose
Charms, "I am dazzled by your charms":
  Ranunculus
Charms, many: Multiflora rose
Charms, "You are radiant with charms":
  Ranunculus
Charms, "Your charms are engraven on my
  heart": Fuchsia
Charms, "Your charms are resplendent": Asiatic ranunculus
Charms, "Your charms are traced upon my heart": Spindle tree
Charms, "Your qualities like your charms are unequaled":
  Peach
Charms, "Your qualities surpass your charms": Mignonette

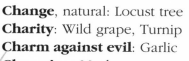

Cross of Jerusalem,
Passion Flower
CHARITY
Yours is without limits

C**HASTITY: Orange blossom.** These flowers are commonly worn
now by the young bride; though we know not why the Orange
blossom was selected as the emblem of Chastity. The custom of wearing
it at weddings, we believe, first originated in France.

Cheerful, always: Coreopsis
Cheerful smile: Coreopsis
Cheerfulness: Buttercup, Chrysanthemum, Crocus
Cheerfulness, in old age: Michaelmas daisy
Childhood: Sweet William
Childhood, "May you ever be pure and lovely": Red rosebud
Childishness: Buttercup
Chivalry: Daffodil
Christian faith: Passion flower
Christian faith, "light of our path": Star of Bethlehem
Claims, "You have no claims": Pulsatilla
Cleanliness: Hyssop, Lovage
Closeness, "Your closeness is welcome": Coriander
Cold, "You are cold": Hydrangea
Cold-hearted: Lettuce
Coldness: Ice plant, Lettuce
Comfort: Lady's mantle

Company, "Great deal is to be gained by good company": Rose in a tuft of grass

Compassion: Allspice, Bergamot, Elder

Compliments, "My compliments": Iris

CONFESSION: **Moss rosebud.** A beautiful and poetical representation of the first confession of love, and so alluded to by our old poets; Rosebuds having for ages been emblems of youthful love.

Confidence: Primrose

Confidence, "Have confidence in me": Primrose

Confidence, in heaven: Canna

Confiding love: Fuchsia

Confused, "I am perplexed": Love-in-a-mist

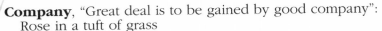

Œillet de Dieu. Oculus Christi.
Je CONFIANCE
la mets en vous.
Carnation of God,
Oculus Christi
CONFIDENCE
I put it in you

CONSOLATION: **Poppy.** Denotes sleep, rest, repose: all of which are well represented in its drowsy properties and influence.

Consolation: Bergamot, Scarlet geranium, Snowdrop

Constancy: Box, Campanula, Blue hyacinth, Ivy, Southernwood

Content: Houstonia

Contract: Straw

Contract, broken: Broken straw

COQUETRY: **Yellow day lily.** Called by the French "the Beauty of a Day"; who reigning, as she generally does, over so many admirers, coquettes with all without loving one.

Coquetry: Dandelion, Daphne

Cordial feelings: Peppermint-scented geranium*

Cordiality: Peppermint

Counterfeit: Mock orange

Courage: Borage, Black poplar, Thyme

Courage, "I admire your courage": Camomile

Craftiness: Sweet William

Crime: Tamarisk

Criticism: Squirting cucumber

CRUELTY: **Stinging nettle.** Wounds the hand that presses it ever so gently. However dull the comprehension of a lover might be, he could not well fail to understand the meaning of this plant.

Cruelty: Marigold, Stinging nettle
Cry, "I cry for you": Elecampane
Cure: Balm, Balm of Gilead
Cure, to cure: Yarrow
Cure, for heartache: Cranberry, Yarrow
Curiosity: Sycamore

Daintiness: Aster
Dance, "Your hand for the next quadrille?": Ivy geranium
Dance, "I engage you for the next dance": Ivy
Dandy: Cuckoo flower
Danger: Rhododendron
Daughter, beloved: Cinquefoil
Death: Cypress
Death, "I change but in dying": Bay leaf
Death, "I will not survive you": Mulberry tree
Death, "My best days are past": Autumn crocus
Death, "My feelings will change only with death": Bay
Death, natural change: Locust tree
Death, preferable to loss of innocence: Dried white rose
Death, sleep of the heart: White poppy
Death, "You will be my death": Hemlock
Decide, "Allow me time to decide": Goldenrod

DECEIT: **White catchfly.** This white flower may be found in almost every sandy field in June; and many a poor fly that is attracted to it by its odour, finds death amid its entangling leaves.

Deceit: Bugloss, Mock orange, Monkshood, Sweet rocket, Venus's fly-trap

DECEITFUL CHARMS: **Thorn apple.** A gorgeous shrub, scarcely equalled in beauty, although its perfume is considered unhealthy; hence its meaning in floral language.

Deceitful hope: Daffodil

Deceive, "Do not deceive yourselves": Saffron

DECLARATION OF LOVE: **Tulip.** So received: though far inferior to the Rosebud as an emblem of the tender passion.

Dejection: Lupine

Delay: Feverfew

DELICACY: **Bluebottle.** A beautiful flower that grows in the cornfields, and is second to none in the delicacy of its colouring.

Delicacy: Bluebell, Cornflower, Lily of the valley

Delicateness, "Delicate and lonely as this flower": Wood hyacinth

✓**Departure**: Sweet pea

DESERTION: **Love-lies-a-bleeding.** Like the Forget-me-not, conveys a meaning in its very name.

Desertion: Columbine

DESIRE: **Jonquil, or Poet's Narcissus.** The White Jonquil, or Poet's Narcissus, is found in most gardens, and is well known by the rich crimson rim which marks the golden cup in its centre. Although linked with the old heathen mythology, the name of the foolish youth, who became enamoured of his own shadow, as he saw it reflected in the waters, still this poetical flower is allied to our true English family of Daffodils, and is often mentioned by our early dramatists. It might have been turned to better use, in floral language, than it is; but being just admissible, and not requiring any over-exertion of fancy to see that Narcissus had a Desire to love some one who resembled himself, we must allow it to pass. The White Jonquil possesses the sweetest perfumes which breathe from the sweet and parted lips of May.

Desire: Red rose

Despair: Cypress, Marigold and Cypress

Despair, "Do not despair": Petunia

Despair, "I am in despair": Withered white rose

Despair, "I have lost all": Scabiosa

Desperation: Snapdragon

Destiny, "My destiny is in your hands": Camellia

Devoted, generous and devoted love: Honeysuckle

DEVOTED AFFECTION: **Honeysuckle, or Woodbine.** A beautiful adaptation of a sweet wild flower to a poetical sentence, and called by the French the "Links of Love", from its clinging to the object it adorns.

Devoted affection: Heliotrope

DEVOTED ATTACHMENT: **Heliotrope.** The heliotrope, in floral language, is dedicated to Devoted Attachment, a meaning synonymous to that given to our English Woodbine or Honeysuckle, in the language of flowers: it is a native of Peru, and might be well spared from our Alphabet of Love. Its smell is very overpowering in a close room, and as such considered unhealthy. We know no legend connected with it, nor any poem that has been written in its praise; we even doubt whether it possesses the quality from which it was named—that of turning towards the sun, both when it rose and set.

Devotion: Heliotrope, Lavender
Devotion, sincere: Nutmeg thyme*
Die, "We die together": Gathered flowers
Difficulty: Hawthorn
Difficulty, "I surmount difficulties": Mistletoe
Diffidence: Cyclamen
Dignity: Clove, Elm
Dignity, and elegance: Dahlia
Dignity, of mind: Hundred-leaved rose
Disappointed expectation: Fish geranium

Capucine, Reine Marguerite.
DÉVOUEMENT
Il est sans bornes.
Nasturtium,
Queen Daisy
DEVOTION
It is without limits

DISAPPOINTED LOVE: **Willow.** Shakespeare made Othello's maid, poor Barbara, go about the house hanging her head aside, and singing, "Oh, willow, willow!" for he she loved proved false.

Disappointment: Mock orange
Discouraged, "I shall not be discouraged": Burdock burr
Discretion: Lemon blossom, Maidenhair
Disdain: Yellow chrysanthemum, Yellow carnation, Rue
Dislike: Monkshood
Dislike, "I can't stand you": Garlic
Dislike, "I find your presumptions laughable": Dandelion
Displeasure: Wormwood
Dissension: Pride of China, "The stalk from which the flower is broken off"

Distinction: Cardinal flower, Scarlet lobelia
Distrust: Lavender
Divinity, "You are my divinity": Cowslip
Docility: Rush
Domestic happiness: Holly
Domestic industry: Flax
Domestic virtues: Sage

D OUBT: **Apricot blossom.** Which requires gentle rains, and warm, bright, sunshiny weather, to bring the fruit to perfection.

Dream, "I dreamed of thee": Thorn apple
Dream, of a lover: Southernwood
Duplicity: Manchineel
Durability: Dogwood
Duration: Cornelian cherry

Easter, symbol of: Pussy willow
Ecstasy, transport: Cape jasmine (Gardenia)
Education, love of learning: Cinnamon basil*
Education, good: Cherry tree
Egotism: Narcissus

E LEGANCE: **Acacia.** There is something about the form of these beautiful flowers, as they droop and wave in the breeze, that conveys an idea of elegance and neatness, without being gaudy. They conjure up the image of a lady chastely and not garishly attired.

Elegance: Aster
Elegance, mature and finished: Pomegranate flower
Elevation: Fir tree, Scotch fir
Eloquence: Water lily
Embarrass, "Your attentions only embarrass me": Borage

E NCHANTMENT: **Vervain.** Supposed to have been used by the wizards of old in their spells, omens, etc.; but that power is now transferred to the bewitching face of a woman.

Enchantment: Lemon verbena, Verbena
Encouragement: Goldenrod

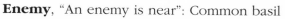

Enemy, "An enemy is near": Common basil
Energy: Red salvia
Energy in adversity: Camomile
Enjoyable activity: Lemon thyme
Ennui: Moss

ENVY: **Bramble.** Tears and rends every thing it can cling to, and is the dread of fair ladies who venture to ruralise in old forests, thick with underwood. The Briar and Thorn are old emblems of Pain, Envy, and Suffering, and are frequently alluded to by our poets.

Envy: Crane's bill geranium
Escape: Pennyroyal

ESTEEM: **Sage.** So called, no doubt, in floral language, because the sages and philosophers of old were held in high esteem for their gravity and wisdom.

Esteem: Strawberry tree
Esteem, "I claim, at least, your esteem": Potentilla
Esteem, "I esteem, but do not love you": Spiderwort
Evil, charm against: Garlic
Evil, unite against: Scarlet verbena
Evil, ward off: Santolina
Excellence, unpretending: Camellia
Excessive sensibility: Aspen tree
Expectation: Anemone (Windflower)
Extravagance, fantastic: Scarlet poppy
Eyes, beautiful: Variegated tulip
Eyes, sunbeamed: Scarlet lychnis

Facility: Germander
Fair, ever: Monthly rose
Fair, "She is fair": Gillyflower
Fair, "You are fair and fascinating": White or variegated pink
Fairie's fire: Pyrus japonica
Faith, light of our path: Star of Bethlehem
Faith, Christian: Passion flower

Faith, "Pray for me": White verbena
Faith, sacred affections: Calendula
Faithful, "Accept a faithful heart": Weigela
Faithful, incense of a faithful heart: Frankincense
Faithfulness: Germander, Heliotrope, Lavender, Blue violet

F ALSEHOOD: **Deadly nightshade.** The fruit of which produces poison and death, and cannot be pointed out too soon to the innocent and unwary, that they may be prevented from gathering it.

Falsehood: Bugloss, Yellow lily
Fame: Tulip tree
Fame, "I overcome everything", "I rise above all": Mistletoe
Fame, "Fame speaks him great and good": Apple blossom
Family union: Pink verbena
Farewell: Michaelmas daisy, Spruce pine
Farewell, "I miss you": Balsam
Fascinating, "You are fair and fascinating": White or variegated pink
Fascination: Enchanter's nightshade, Fern, Honesty
Fascination, "You have bewitched me": Lemon verbena
Fashionable, "She will be fashionable": Queen's rocket
Fastidiousness: Purple lilac
Fastidiousness, "Don't make such a to-do about small things": Mint
Fate: Flax
Fate, "The color of my fate": Coral honeysuckle
Feast: Parsley
Fecundity: Hollyhock
Feeling, delicacy of: Lemon verbena
Festivity: Parsley
Fickleness: Pink larkspur
Fickleness, likely to change frequently without reason: Wild honeysuckle
Fidelity: White chrysanthemum, Costmary, Honeysuckle, Ivy, Rosemary, Veronica
Fidelity, female: Veronica
Fidelity, in misfortune: Wallflower
Finesse: Sweet William

Liseron-Pois éternel
FIDÉLITÉ
Elle ne se démentira jamais.

Hedge Bells,
Eternal Pea
FIDELITY
It never belies itself

Fire: Fraxinella (Gas plant)

FIRST EMOTIONS OF LOVE: Lilac. Its fragrance, and the fresh and healthy look of its blossoms, which are amongst the first to unfold in the spring, are well chosen as the representatives of early love.

Fitness {suitability}: Sweet flag
Flame: Red iris
Flame of love: Yellow iris
Flattery: Fennel, Venus's looking-glass
Flee away: Pennyroyal
Folly: Columbine
Foolishness: Pomegranate
Foppishness {affection}: Pomegranate
Forbidden, "It is forbidden": Privet

FORESIGHT: Dandelion. The schoolboy's clock and oracle in every village: for who, when young, has not blown its tufted down away, and at every breath sent a wish after the feathered seeds of the Dandelion?

Foresight: Holly, Strawberry
Forever thine: Dahlia
Forget, "Let us forget": Yellow rose
Forget me not: Forget-me-not, Heartsease
Forgetfulness: Lunaria, White poppy
Forgotten, "Am I forgotten?": Holly

FORSAKEN: Primrose. We have selected the Primrose in honour of Milton, who says, "And the rathe Primrose that *forsaken* dies"; and for the sake of the Bard of Paradise such a meaning ought it ever to bear, instead of the Anemone.

Forsaken: Lilac, Chinese rose, Weeping willow
Fortune, pride of newly acquired: Primrose
Fraternal affection: Mock orange
Fraternal love: Woodbine
Freeze, "Your looks freeze me": Ice plant
Freshness, of complexion: Damask rose
Friendliness: Spearmint

FRIENDSHIP: **Ivy.** Denotes something true and lasting, and not to be changed by the beating of the winter winds. It is a much better emblem of Friendship than the Acacia, which some have chosen.

Friendship: Acacia, Acacia rose, Balsam, Cedar, Yellow rose

Friendship, early and sincere: Periwinkle

Friendship, flower: Marigold

Friendship, "Great deal is to be gained by good company": Rose in a tuft of grass

Friendship, "I rejoice in your friendship": Yellow rose

Friendship, "I will always be true": Azalea

Friendship, in adversity: Snowdrop

Friendship, "My time with you is a pleasure": Lemon thyme*

Friendship, true: Oak-leaf scented geranium

Friendship, unchanging: Arbor vitae

Friendship, warm: Pine

Friendship, warms old hearts: Chervil

Friendship, "You light up my life": Feverfew*

Friendship, "Your friendship is pleasing and agreeable to me": Glycine

Frivolity: London pride

Frown: Peony

Frugality: Endive, Succory

Fruitfulness: Hollyhock

Future, foretelling the future: Yarrow

Periwinkle, Honeysuckle
FRIENDSHIP
Love me like I love you

Gaiety: Butterfly flower

Gallantry: Bouquet of flowers, Nosegay, Sweet William

Game: Hyacinth

Generosity: Orange tree

Generous and devoted love: Honeysuckle

Genius: Plane tree, Acanthus

Genteel: Rose

Gentility: Scented-leaf geranium

Gentle, "She is fair": Gillyflower

Gentle, "You are gentle, graceful, lovely": Pink rose

Gentleness: Baby's breath

Girl, young: Rosebud

Girl, "Young girl passing from childhood to youth": Primrose

Gladness: Coreopsis, Frankincense, Myrrh, Sweet cicely

GLORY: Laurel. Was used by the ancients to crown those heroes who returned from the wars victorious. Chaucer, our oldest English poet, says, "He rode home crown'd with laurel, like a conqueror."

Glory: Bay wreath, Hickory, Mountain laurel, Coral rose

Glory, "I overcome everything": Mistletoe

Good luck: White heather

Good news: Viburnum

Good spirits: Dill

Good wishes: Basil, Holly

Goodness: Good King Henry

Goodness, gentle: Strawberry-scented geranium

Goodness, perfect: Strawberry

Grace: Hundred-leaved rose, Multiflora rose, Pink rose, Rue

Grace and elegance: Yellow jasmine

Graceful, "You are gentle, graceful, lovely": Pink rose

Gracefulness: Birch tree

Grandeur: Ash tree, Beech tree

Alcée.
Elle BONTÉ *enchaine les cœurs.*
Holly-Hock
GOODNESS
It chains the hearts

GRATITUDE: Agrimony. A sweet, lowly plant, adorned with small, beautiful, golden-colored flowers, that upcone like a pile of stars. It is greatly valued by the herb-gatherers in the country, and considered by many to make much better tea than half of the rubbish which is sold under that name.

Gratitude: Campanula

Gratitude, "My gratitude exceeds your care": Dahlia

Grave, affection beyond the grave: Locust tree

Greed: Primrose

GRIEF OR PAIN: Marigold. Often alluded to by our ancient poets, as bowing its head and mourning for the absence of the sun.

Grief: Aloe, Calendula, Campanula, Marigold, Rue

Grief, overcoming, "I rise above all": Mistletoe
Guiding star, "Your love is my guiding star": Angelica

Happiness: Mugwort, Oregano, Thyme
Happiness, domestic: Holly
Happiness, "I am too happy": Gardenia
Happiness, joy and: Wild marjoram
Happiness, "May happiness be yours": Red and white rose
Happiness, "Remember our happiness": Silver-leaf thyme*
Happiness, return of: Lily of the valley
Happiness, rural: Tulip tree, Yellow violet
Happiness, happy thoughts: Heartsease
Happiness, transient: Spiderwort
Happiness, warms old hearts: Chervil

HAPPY RETIREMENT: **Wild harebell.** The Harebell we have already alluded to as belonging to the order of Campanula, and it has been well chosen, in floral language, as the emblem of Happy Retirement. It is one of the most beautiful of all our Autumn wildflowers, adorning the sides of woods and shady places with its delicate bells of blue, clear and pure as ever hung upon the azure face of heaven.

Hardiness: Cranberry
Hardness: Bedstraw
Hate, "I can't stand you": Garlic
Hatred: Common basil, Fumitory
Haughtiness: Amaryllis, Larkspur, Tall sunflower
Heal, "I wound to heal": Eglantine rose (Sweet briar)
Healing: Balm of Gilead, Betony
Health: Horehound, Iceland moss, Yarrow
Health, good: Sage
Heartache, "Alas, for my heart": Red chrysanthemum
Heartache, cure for: Celandine
Heartless, "You are heartless": Hydrangea
Heaven: Delphinium
Heaven, confidence in: Canna
Heedlessness: Flowering almond

Hermitage: Milkwort
High-souled: Magnolia
Home: Myrtle
Homeliness: Mint
Honesty: Honesty

HOPE: **Hawthorn.** The beautiful Hawthorn has been selected, as well as the Snowdrop, for the emblem of Hope: and there are few but can recall with delight the healthy fragrance which has cheered them, while wandering between the green hedgerows of England. Our old poets, as if despairing to find a fitting name for the fragrant blossom, have called it May, after one of the pleasantest months in the whole year.

Hope: Flowering almond
Hope, "Do not despair": Petunia
Hope, extinguished: Convolvulus major
Hope, in adversity: Norway spruce
Hope, in love: Bachelor button
Hope, pleasures of: Crocus
Hopeless, not heartless: Love-lies-a-bleeding
Horror: Serpentine cactus

Bouton de Rose ·Renoncule.
ESPÉRANCE
Ranimez mon espoir.
Rose bud, Ranunculus
HOPE
Revive my hope

HOSPITALITY: **Oak.** In former days the ancients were wont to entertain their guests beneath a tree. Under the oak of Mamre, Abraham welcomed the angels.

Hostile thoughts: Tansy
Humanity: Marsh mallow, Oak leaf

HUMILITY: **Broom.** The "Bonny Broom" is familiar to every lover of the country, and cannot be mistaken for the gorse or furze, even in the dark; for, although their flowers are very similar, there is a difference in the latter, which is soon "felt". The Broom is one of England's oldest flowers, and was as familiar to the eye of the ancient Briton as it is to our own.

Humility: Field lily, Small white bindweed
Hush!: Belladonna

Violette ·Coréopsis
HUMILITÉ
Plus je m'humilie, plus je m'élève.
Violet, Coreopsis
HUMILITY
The more humble I am,
the more I elevate

I

ILL NATURE: **Crab blossom.** "As sour as a crab" has long been an old English saying, hence its signification.

Illness, "I will suffer all for you": Sage
Illness, "I wound to heal": Eglantine rose
Imagination: Lupine

IMMORTALITY: **Amaranth.** One of the flowers which was fabled to grow in the gardens of the gods. Milton mentions it amongst those which blow in heavy, and makes the angels in their adoration cast down

> *Their crowns inwove with amaranth and gold:*
> *Immortal amaranth, a flower which once,*
> *In Paradise, fast by the tree of life,*
> *Began to bloom, but soon, for man's offence,*
> *To heaven removed.*

Immortality: Amaranth, Arbor vitae, Tansy

IMPATIENCE: **Balsam.** Which when touched is said to throw the seeds out of the capsules with great force; and from this quality it is selected to express irritation or ingratitude.

Impatience: Impatiens
Importunate, "I am never importunate": Rose leaf
Impatient resolves: Red balsam
Inconstancy: Evening primrose, Wild honeysuckle
Incorruptibility: Cedar
Indecision: Goldenrod

INDEPENDENCE: **Wild-plum blossom.** One of the oldest and hardiest of our English forest fruits, which grows wild in hundreds of hedges, and cannot be trained in gardens or orchards. It seems to love best those rugged and solitary nooks which have never been cultivated by the hand of man since the creation, and is well chosen as an emblem of Independence.

Independence: Plum tree, White oak
Indifferent, "I am perfectly indifferent to you": Dogwood

INDIFFERENCE: **Candytuft.** So it stands in all floral alphabets, because its blossoms are scentless.

Indiscretion: Feathery reed
Industry: Red clover
Industry, domestic: Flax
Infidelity: Yellow rose
Ingenuousness: White pink

INGRATITUDE: **Buttercup.** So called in the Language of Flowers, because it is supposed to injure the cattle that feed upon it; and no honey can be gathered from the gaudy gold of its flowers.

Ingratitude: Thornless rose, Cuckoo flower
Injustice: Hop

INNOCENCE: **Daisy.** The Daisy was Chaucer's favourite flower. His is the adoration of a heart which overflowed with love for the Daisy. His song was ever ready to burst out anew as he exclaimed, "Oh, the Daisy, it is sweet!" Paying lowly reverence to this old English flower he happily called it "The Eye of Day".

Rose blanche. Lis.
INNOCENCE
Vous êtes son image.

White Rose, Lily
INNOCENCE
You are his image

Innocence: Rosebud, White violet
Innocence, maidenly: Sweet marjoram
Insincerity: Foxglove

INSINUATION: **Bindweed, or Larger convolvulus.** Which forces its way through every open space it can find between the branches, until you can scarcely discover another leaf besides its own, so closely are its long, trailing stems twisted along the boughs it has insinuated itself amongst.

Inspiration: Angelica
Instability: Dahlia
Instruction: Bayberry
Intellect: Black walnut
Intellectual excellence: Sumac
Interest: Savory
Interest, lasting: Tarragon
Intoxicated with pleasure: Heliotrope
Intoxication: Heliotrope, Vine
Inutility: Meadowsweet

J

Jealousy: Yellow chrysanthemum, French marigold, [ ]
  Yellow rose
Jest: Southernwood
Joy: Burnet, Calendula, Gardenia, Germander, Marigold,
  Marjoram, Oregano, Parsley, Yellow rose, Saffron crocus
Joy and happiness: Wild marjoram
Joy on the mountain: Oregano
Justice: Rudbeckia
Justice, "Do me justice": Chestnut tree
Justice, "Justice shall be done you": Coltsfoot
Justice, "We will do you justice": Sweet-scented coltsfoot
Justice, "You shall have justice": Sweet-scented tussilage

K

Kindness: Blue bell
Kindness, "I feel your kindness": Flax
Kindness, frozen: Horehound
Knowledge, useful: Parsley

L

Lamentation: Aspen tree

LASTING BEAUTY: Stock, or Gillyflower. For the latter is the old
name of this truly English flower, which our ancestors also called July
flower. It flourished in the gardens of the old baronial castles hundreds of
years ago, and time and cultivation have rather added to, than diminished
its beauty: and it is, therefore, well deserving of the appellation of Lasting
Beauty.

Laughter: Saffron crocus
Learning, love of: Cinnamon basil*
Levity: Larkspur, Daily rose
Liberty: Oak
Life: Lucerne
Life, everlasting: Tansy
Life, long: Sage
Life, tree of life: Arbor vitae

Light of our path: Star of Bethlehem

Lightness: Larkspur

Live for me: Arbor vitae

Lonely, "delicate and lonely as this flower": Wood hyacinth

Longevity: Fig

Loss, "I have lost all": Honeyflower

LOVE: **Myrtle.** The Myrtle had its birth in the sunny clime of the East, and first grew amid those gardens where the dark-eyed daughters of the sun, as they floated through the lazy circles of the dreamy dance, shook out their silken ringlets to the dallying wind. In many a peaceful valley which nestles down between the mountain-passes it is found, with its beautiful white blossoms blowing amid the untrodden solitudes, and filling the air with fragrance for miles around. The fair maidens of Judea bore it in their processions, and twined its scented branches into green arbours at their solemn festivals. And among the ancient traditions of the Arabs it is recorded, that Adam bore in his hand a sprig of Myrtle, when he was driven from the garden of paradise—it might be from the very bower where he first breathed his love into the ear of Eve.

Love: Sweet basil, Red chrysanthemum, Heliotrope, Pansy, Rose, Violet

Love, addicting, "Your love is addicting": Nutmeg

Love, ambassador of: Cabbage rose

Love, at first sight: Chervil, Coreopsis

Love, bashful: Pink-flowered damask rose

Love, "Be my love": Myrtle

Love, bonds of: Honeysuckle

Love, chaste: Acacia

Love, confiding: Fuchsia

Love, concealed: Yellow acacia

Love, conjugal: Linden tree, Lime tree

Love, constant: Box

Love, consumed by: Hibiscus

Love, dangerous, "Love is dangerous": Carolina rose

Love, declaration of: Red tulip

Love, decrease, "The decrease of love, on better acquaintance": Yellow rose

Love, estranged: Lotus flower

Love, eternal: Heliotrope

Love, everlasting: Baby's breath

Love, everlasting, "I change but in dying": Bay leaf

Love, filial: Virgin's bower

Love, first emotions of: Purple lilac

Love, at first sight: Coreopsis

Love, forsaken: Anemone

Love, fraternal: Woodbine

Love, fruits of: Rosehips

Love, generous and devoted: Honeysuckle

Love, genuine, "My love is genuine": Lavender rose

Fl de Grenade Cupidome
AMOUR
Qui vous connait vous aime·
Flower of Granada,
Cupidome
LOVE
He who knows
you, loves you

Love, gifts of: Carolina allspice

Love, happy: Bridal rose

Love, hope in: Cornflower

Love, "I love": Red chrysanthemum

Love, "I love you": Heliotrope, Red rose

Love, "If you do love me, you will find me out": Maiden's blush rose

Love, hopeless: Yellow tulip

Love, in absence: Myrtle

Love, in idleness: Heartsease

Love, intoxication with: Catnip

Love, maternal: Moss

Love, maternal, "I live for thee": Cedar

Love, memory of: Cedar

Love, morning, "I, with the morning's love, have oft made sport": Cornflower (Bachelor button)

Love, Mother's: Dianthus

Love, passionate: Passion flower

Love, platonic: Acacia

Love, positive: Myrtle

Love, pretended: Catchfly

Love, pure: Single pink, Lavender rose

Love, pure and ardent: Carnation

Love, returned: Ambrosia

Love, returned, "I partake of {share} your sentiments": Double pink

Love, returned, "I reciprocate your affection": Feverfew

Love, returned, "I share your sentiments": Daisy

Love, secret, "I love you in secret": Gardenia

Love, secret untold: Gardenia

Love, self: Narcissus

Love, slighted: Yellow chrysanthemum

Love, "Speak low if you speak love": Honeyflower

Love, steadfast: Camellia

Love, ties of: Honeysuckle

Love, too young to: White rosebud

Love, trap, "I fall into the trap laid for me": White catchfly

Love, true: Forget-me-not

Love, true, "I live for thee": Cedar

Love, true, "I will always be true": Azalea

Love, undiminished by adversity: Dogwood

Love, unending, "My feelings will change only with death": Bay

Love, unfading: Globe amaranth

Love, wedded: Ivy

Love, without, heart ignorant of love: White rosebud

Love, without, heart that knows not love: White rosebud

Love, without, "I admire but cannot love you": Bay

Love, without, "I find your presumptions laughable": Dandelion

Love, without, "You have no claims": Pulsatilla

Love, woman's: Red pink

Love, "You light up my life": Feverfew*

Love, youthful: Red catchfly

Love of learning: Cinnamon basil*

Love of nature: Magnolia

Love of variety: China aster

Loveliness: Chrysanthemum, Pompom rose

Loveliness, "Your qualities surpass your loveliness": Mignonette

Lovely, always: Double pink

Lovely, "Thou art very lovely": Austrian rose

Lovely, "You are gentle, graceful, lovely": Pink rose

Lovely, "You will always be lovely": China pink

L OVE'S CAPTIVE: **Peach-blossom.** Every one who has beheld the
rich bloom of the Peach must have been captivated by its beauty,
whether seen on the velvet cheek of the fruit, or the delicate hue of its
blossoms.

Loyalty: Lavender, Rosemary, Blue violet
Loyalty, "I will always be true": Azalea
Luck: Lavender
Luck, good: White heather
Luck, "You are lucky": Four-leaf clover
Lull: Dill
Luxury: Chestnut

Magic: Angelica
Maidenly innocence: Sweet marjoram
Majesty: Lily
Majesty and power: Crown imperial
Malevolence: Scarlet lobelia
Manners: Rue
Marriage: Ivy, Saffron crocus
Maternal care: Coltsfoot

M ATERNAL LOVE: **Moss.** The soft, green, velvet covering of many a
spot which would otherwise be brown and barren; it grows around
and shelters the stem of many a delicate flower, which would otherwise
perish, and gives warmth to many a chilly nook; and so may fancy
stretch, link by link, until it traces in it a resemblance of Maternal Love.

Matrimony: Ivy, Linden tree
Meeting, an appointed meeting: Everlasting pea
Meeting, expected: Nutmeg-scented geranium
Meeting, unexpected: Lemon-scented geranium
Melancholy: Dead leaves, Weeping willow
Melancholy spirit: Night-smelling geranium
Memory: Mock orange
Memory, love's: Red bay
Memory, pleasures of: Periwinkle
Mental beauty: Clematis, Kennedia, Virgin's bower

Merit: Bay

Merit, hidden: Coriander

Merit, superior: Moss rose

Merit, unpatronized: Rose-colored primrose

Merry, "You are merry": Rosa mundi

Merry heart: Burnet

Message: Blue iris

Message, "I have a message for you": Iris

Messenger: Blue iris

Messengers, love's: Campion rose

Mildness: Privet

Mine, "Be mine!": Four-leaf clover

Mirth: Crocus, Wild grape

Misanthropy: Thistle, Teasel

Misery, the heart's misery: Crimson heart primrose

Misuse, "Don't misuse me": Lemon balm

Moaning: Trembling poplar

MODESTY: **Blue violet.** Every one can remember some bank on which the Violet blows—some green land or pleasant foot-path in which they have been stopped in spring by its fragrance. "Sweet Violet" is one of the earliest cries which greet the ear in spring, telling us that they have come again, like beautiful children, heralding in the approach of summer, they bring joyous tidings of brighter days, and the return of singing birds and the whispers of long leaves and pleasant walks, reminding us that Nature has awoke from her slumber, and is shaking open the unblown buds, which have gathered around her during her long winter's sleep. Dear was this modest and beautiful flower to the hearts of our elder poets, and from its sweetness, buried amid the broad green leaves, they drew forth many an exquisite image and in it found the emblems of hidden Virtue, and neglected Modesty, and unchanging Love.

Modesty: White violet

Modesty, feminine: Calla

Modesty, modest worth: Sweet woodruff

Money, in both pockets: Honesty

Morals: Rue

Mother, maternal care: Coltsfoot

Mother, maternal love: Moss

Mother, Mother's Day emblem: Dianthus
Mother, mother's love: Dianthus
Mother, mother's protection: Lady's mantle
Mourning: Cypress, Weeping willow

Music: Reeds. Pan, the god of Shepherds, is said to have first formed the Arcadian pipes from Reeds, which he called Cyrinz, in honour of a beautiful nymph who was changed into a Reed.

Music: Quaking oats

Nature, love of: Magnolia
Neatness: Birch, Broom
Neglect, "I die if neglected": Viburnum

NEGLECTED BEAUTY: Meadowsweet. My predecessors have been pleased to make this beautiful and fragrant flower, which is called the Queen of the Meadow, and whose perfume is sweet as that of the Hawthorn, the emblem of Uselessness. In contradistinction to the meaning they have assigned to it, I have dared to christen it the "Neglected Beauty"; for a sweeter flower blows not in all the green meadows of pastoral England, and Neglected Beauty it shall ever represent to me, for it has been too long overlooked. Miss Twamley, in her "Wild Flowers", says—and honour to her for saying it—"Its tall, red-tinted stems, handsome jagged leaves, and foam-like flowers, so rich in scent, and so very beautiful, well deserve the title so often bestowed upon it of 'Queen of the Meadows'. The French and Italian names have both the same meaning—'Meadow Queen'. It fills the summer air with a scent like new-mown hay and hawthorn." Fair readers! shall this sweet flower, so admirably advocated by a lady, any longer stand disgraced as the emblem of uselessness, or will you not rather step forward and defend it as a Neglected Beauty, until some happier emblem is chosen? Just fancy one of your own sweet selves, for want of an advocate, so thrown back and insulted!

NEGLECTED LOVE: Laurustinus. The Laurustinus is a beautiful evergreen, bearing white flowers; which, before they become opened, have all the richness of the Rose about the colour of the buds. Why so hardy a plant was selected for that image of Neglected Love we know not, unless it be that Love dies a hard death, and is difficult to destroy.

Night: Convolvulus minor

O

Obstacle: Ox-eye, Rest harrow
Old, "I do not fear to grow old": Autumn crocus
Old age, cheerfulness in: Michaelmas daisy
Old beau: Ice plant
Oracle: Dandelion
Ornament: Yoke elm

P

Pain: Marigold
Pain, "Your presence softens my pain": Milk vetch
Painting: Auricula
Parasite: Mistletoe
Parental affection: Sorrel
Passion: Myrtle
Passion, "Your passion sends blushes to my cheeks": Sweet marjoram

Œillet rouge-Ixia.

ARDEUR
Elle me consume.

Red Carnation, Ixia
PASSION
It consumes me

PATIENCE: **Dock.** The Haunter of every wayside, where it flourishes in spite of dust and every footstep that trampled it down.

Patience: Aster, Ox-eye
Patriotism: American elm, Nasturtium
Peace: Myrtle, Olive tree
Penitence: Yew

PENSIVENESS: **Cowslip.** Called by our old poets the Sweet Nun of the Fields, and immortalized in Shakespeare's "Midsummer Night's Dream".

Perfection, "You are perfect": Pineapple, Strawberry
Perplexity: Love-in-a-mist
Perseverance: Magnolia, Southernwood
Perseverance, "I rise above all": Mistletoe
Persistence: Burdock burr
Pestering, "Stop your pestering": Butterfly weed
Philosophy, time and: Pine
Pity: Camellia, Pine, Black spruce

Play: Hyacinth

Playful gaiety: Day lily

Pleasant company of friends: Lemon balm

Please, desire to: Daphne

Pleasure, delicate: Sweet pea

Pleasure, evanescent: Red poppy

Pleasure, everlasting: Sweet pea

Pleasure, of hope: Crocus

Pleasure, of memory: Periwinkle

Pleasure, "My time with you is a pleasure": Lemon thyme*

Pleasure, without alloy: Moss rose

POETRY: **Eglantine.** I will not pause to inquire why, for Poetry is a thorny sweetness, and those who touch it must not mind a prick or two. Even if the world admire not its flowers, there is a sweetness about its very leaves; and to be nestled near them in a green nook is to enjoy a pleasure which needs no praise to enhance it. As Touchstone says of Audrey, in "As You Like It", "Though a poor thing, it is mine own"; and the Sweet Briar Rose, or Eglantine, has ever been a favourite flower with the English poets. So we accept the emblem for want of a better.

Politeness: Bouquet of flowers

Poor, "We may be poor, but we will be happy": Vernal grass

Poverty: Evergreen

Pray for me: White verbena

Precaution: Goldenrod

Pride: Tall sunflower

Pride, "For once may pride befriend me": Tiger flower

PREFERENCE: **Apple-blossom.** In the Apple-blossom we see the Lily and the Rose blended together, like a blush softening into the snowy whiteness of a sweet face; decking, per adventure, some countenance that we secretly love—a love which, from very fear, we dare not give utterance to, lest some other should already be preferred. It may be, too, that at the same time we already stand high in her estimation, and yet her innate modesty causes her to shrink back from revealing it: and so we go on dallying and sighing together, like the spring breeze playing in and out of a bunch of Apple-blossoms, then quitting them until the warmer air of the bolder summer comes forth, and ripens the blushing blossoms into the full fruit of mellowed love. Of all the beauties which Spring, stepping forth, hangs upon the trees, leaving a wreath here and a garland there, the loveliest of all her rich decorations is still the opening Apple-blossom—the emblem of Preference in Love.

Preference: Rose-scented geranium

Preference, present: Apple-scented geranium

Presumption: Snapdragon

Pretension, "You are without pretension": Pasque-flower anemone

Pretty: Rose

Pride: Amaryllis, Carnation, Scarlet primrose

Pride, of birth: Crown imperial

Profit: Cabbage

Prohibition: Privet

Promise, "keep your promises": Plum tree

Promise, of future wealth: Buttercup

Promptitude: Ten-week stock

Prosperity: Beech tree, Bryony, Wheat

Prosperity, beauty and: English Daisy

Protection: Feverfew, Juniper, Lady's mantle, Santolina

Proud spirit: Gloxinia

Providence: Purple clover

Purification: Rue

Purity: White lily, Lily of the valley, Star of Bethlehem

Purity, and beauty: White lily

Marguerite blanche - Primevère.
CANDEUR
C'est la vertu des âmes pures.

White Daisy, Primrose
PURENESS
It is the virtue
of the pure souls

PURITY OF HEART: **White Water-lily.** The White Water-lily is the Queen of the Waves, and reigns sole sovereign over the streams; and it was a species of Water-lily which the old Egyptians and ancient Indians worshipped—the most beautiful object that was held sacred in their superstitious creed—and one which we cannot look upon even now without feeling a delight mingled with reverence. No flower looks more lovely than this "Lady of the Lake", resting her crowned head on a green throne of velvet.

Purity, "Your purity equals your loveliness": Orange blossom

Queen, "You are the queen of coquettes": Queen's rocket

Quiet, "Hush!": Belladonna

R

Rarity: Mandrake
Readiness: Red valerian
Ready armed: Gladioli
Reason: Goat's rue
Recall: Silver- or grey-leaved geranium
Recluse: Moss
Recantation: Lotus leaf
Recollections, sweet: Periwinkle

Immortelle Camelia
RECONNAISSANCE
Elle sera éternelle.

Immortelle, Camelia
RECOGNITION
It will be forever

RECONCILIATION: **Hazel.** The best way for young lovers to make up a quarrel is to walk into a beautiful wood, and seat themselves upon the flowers under the transparent leaves of the Hazel, for there they will soon become reconciled.

Reconciliation: Filbert, Star of Bethlehem
Refreshment, eternal: Mint

REFUSAL: **Snapdragon.** So called from the closing lips of the flower, which will not open until rudely pressed.

Refusal: White pink
Regard: Daffodil, White rose

REGRETS, **"My regrets follow you to the grave": Asphodel.** A flower that in ancient times was planted around the graves of the dead, and which was supposed to grow in the gardens of Elysium. Its real signification is regret and sorrow for the dead.

Regrets: Raspberry
Rejected, addresses: Ice plant
Release, "Let me go": Butterfly weed
Religion, light of our path: Star of Bethlehem
Religion, "Pray for me": White verbena
Religion, sacred affections: Calendula
Religious superstition: Aloe, Passion flower
Remember, "Forget me not": Forget-me-not, Heartsease
Remember, "I miss you": Balsam
Remember, "I think of you": Blue salvia

Remember, "I will think of it": Field daisy, Single pink

Remember me: Forget-me-not

Remember our happiness: Silver-leaf thyme*

Remembered, always: Strawflower

Remembrance: Calendula, Marigold, Rosemary

Remembrance, never ceasing: Everlastings

Reminiscences, pleasing: Periwinkle

Remorse: Raspberry

Repentance: Rue

Forget-Me-Not,
Red Immortelle
REMEMBRANCE
I will never
forget you

REPOSE: Convolvulus. The Convolvulus, or Bindweed, is known to every one; from the pale pink flower that clings to the reeds or corn, to the long festoons which throw their large, white, hollow cups over every hedgerow. The Blue convolvulus, which we see so commonly twined around doorporches, and beneath windowsills, constantly closes its flowers about four o'clock, and such a regular "go-to-bed", as it is called in the country, is no bad emblem of Repose.

Reserve: Maple tree

Resistance: Tansy, Tremella

Resolved to win: Purple columbine

Restfulness: Myrtle

Retirement: Maple tree

Retirement, happy: Campanula

RETURN OF HAPPINESS: Lily of the Valley. Lily of the Valley! what a spring sound there is in its very name! How delicate it is, both in form and fragrance; resting its white, fairy-like bells upon a deep background of green. Pleasant visions does it recall before mine eyes of other days—of springs which have long since passed away and sweet woodland spots that were strewn everywhere full "ankle-deep with Lilies of the Valley". They have ever seemed to us as the sweetest and fairest daughters of Spring—the little fairies of the wood, just wakening from their winter sleep.

Revenge: Milk vetch

Reverie: Flowering fern

Revive, "Your presence revives me": Rosemary

Reward of merit: Bay wreath, Crown of roses

Riches: Buttercup, Corn, Wheat
Riches, desire of: King-cup
Riches, false: Sunflower
Rigor: Lantana
Rivalry: Rocket
Romance: Azalea
Roughness of manners: Borage

R UDENESS: **Burdock.** It is a favourite amusement amongst country girls to pelt their rustic swains with the burdock, and that coat must be very threadbare to which they will not adhere. It is a rude and rustic way of making love.

Rural happiness: Tulip tree, Yellow violet

Sacred affections: Calendula
Sacrifice: Hyssop

S ADNESS: **Withered leaves.** An apt emblem in love as well as in nature, telling us that the beauty and brightness of summer is departed.

Sadness: White rose
Safety: Rock rose
Satire: Pepper plant, Prickly pear cactus
Scandal: Hellebore
Sculpture: Hoya
Self-love: Narcissus
Selfishness: Narcissus
Sensibility: White jasmine, Verbena
Sensitiveness: Mimosa, Sensitive plant
Sentiment, light and frivolous: London pride
Separation: Carolina jasmine, Trumpet flower
Serenade: Dew plant
Serious intentions: Sweet basil
Shame, bashful: Peony, Deep-red rose
Sharing, unselfish: Tarragon
Sharpness: Berberry, Lantana

Shy: Peony

Sickness: Anemone, Mimosa

SILENCE: **White Rose.** The White Rose has long been considered as sacred to Silence: over whatever company it was suspended, no secrets were ever revealed, for it hung only above the festal board of sworn friendship. No matter how deep they might drink, or how long the wine-cup might circulate round the table, so long as the White Rose hung over their heads, every secret was considered inviolable; no matter how trivial, or how important the trust, beneath that flower it was never betrayed, for around it was written the sentence: "He who doth secrets reveal beneath my roof shall never live."

Fleurs des champs.
Ceat la SIMPLICITÉ
la vertu des belles ames.

Field Flowers,
Wild Flowers
SIMPLICITY
It is the virtue of
the beautiful souls

Silence: Belladonna, Foxglove, Lotus flower
Silliness: Cockscomb
Simplicity: Daisy, Sweet briar, Wild rose
Simplicity, delicate: Lily of the valley
Simplicity, and beauty: Burgundy rose

SINCERITY: **Fern.** The very name of the Fern calls up the forest, where it still lives on, though ages ago the mighty oaks have been felled— there it still spreads, true to its native soil, the hardy image of deep-rooted Sincerity. It is associated with our oldest fairy legends. Our simple ancestors believed that they had but to find the true "Fern seed", and carry it about with them, to become invisible. What would not a fond lover give for a packet of this fabulous seed, that he might at any hour steal unperceived into the presence of his mistress? But alas! the secret was carried away with the fairies, when they were driven, with bell, book, and candle, from the green and daisied meadows of merry England.

Sincerity: Chervil, Honesty
Single, "I would be single": White rose
Single blessedness: Bachelor button
Singularity: Cockscomb
Skepticism: Nightshade
Skill: Spider orhrys
Slander: Stinging nettle
Sleep, of the heart: White poppy
Smile: Sweet William

Aubépine-Pensée.
Mes lèvres SINCERITÉ
sont d'accord avec mon cœur.

Hawthorn, Pansy
SINCERITY
My lips are in
accord with my heart

Smile, "Lady, deign to smile": Oak-leaf geranium

Smile, cheerful: Coreopsis

SNARE: White catchfly. This white flower may be found in almost every sandy field in June; and many a poor fly that is attracted to it by its odour, finds death amid its entangling leaves.

Snare: Dragon plant

Social intercourse: Lemon balm

SOLITUDE: Heath. The Heath was well chosen as the emblem of Solitude. It could scarcely be otherwise, adorning as it does, the lonely waste, and waving over weary miles of desolate moorland. The Heath recalls scenes of solitude and of silence—vast plains of immeasurable extent.

Solitude: Lichen

SORROW: Yew. One of the oldest monuments our ancestors erected above the dead.

Sorrow: Elecampane, Purple hyacinth, Lupine, Marigold

Sorrow, acute: Aloe

Sorrow, that mourns: Cypress

Sorrowful remembrances: Adonis

South: Foxglove

Spell: Witch hazel

Spice, "Add spice to your life": Oregano*

Spiciness: Savory

Splendor: Lily, Scarlet nasturtium, Sumac

Sport: Hyacinth

Spiritual beauty: Cherry tree blossom

Spouse, "Find a spouse of your own age and background": Mint

Stateliness: Foxglove

Stoicism: Box

Strength: Cedar tree, Fennel

Strength of character: Gladiolus

Student, serious: Cinnamon basil

Stupidity: Scarlet geranium

Fleur d'Oranger-Girofleé.
C'est le DONCEUR *lien des âmes.*

Orange Flower,
Gilliflower
SOFTNESS
It is the goodness
of the souls

Submission: Campanula, Grass

Success, "I overcome everything", "I surmount difficulties": Mistletoe

Success, "May success crown your wishes": Crown vetch

Success, pride of newly acquired fortune: Primrose

Success, resolved to win: Purple columbine

Superstition: Saint John's Wort

Support, "Be my support": Buckbean

Surprise: Betony

Susceptibility: Passion flower

Suspicion: Lavender, Mushroom

Sweet disposition: Honeysuckle, Mallow

Sweet virtues: Bergamot

Sweetness: Costmary, White lily, Vanilla, Blue violet

Sweets to the sweet: Daphne

SYMPATHY: **Thrift.** A good old English name, which means more than can be expressed in half-a-dozen words, and ought never to be forgotten by young lovers; for thriftiness brings comfort, independence, and every thing which, with love, makes life happy; and should misfortune come, it meets with more sympathy than idleness and extravagance.

Sympathy: Bergamot, Sea thrift

Sympathy, "I partake of {share} your sentiments": Daisy, Double pink

Sympathy, "I will suffer all for you": Sage

Talent: White pink

Tartness: Berberry

TASTE: **Fuchsia.** The Fuchsia we leave to the florist; neither its name, nor the quality it is chosen to represent, have any English sound about them.

Temptation: Apple, Quince

Thankfulness: Agrimony

Think of me: Cedar, Red clover, Heartsease

THOUGHT: **Pansy.** "There is Pansies," said the sweet Ophelia; "that's for thoughts": but whether sad or pleasing the immortal poet mentions not. For well did he know that where so many hues were thrown upon the face of one flower, Fancy would, according to the feeling of the moment, trace out her own favourite image. All the old legends which were known about the Pansy in ancient days are lost; saving the one preserved by Shakspere [sic], and woven into his inimitable "Midsummer Night's Dream".

Thoughtlessness: Flowering almond
Thoughts: Pansy
Thoughts, dark: Nightshade
Thoughts, happy: Heartsease
Thoughts, lofty and pure: Tall sunflower
Thoughts, tender and pleasant: Pansy
Thoughts, "Think of me": Cedar, Red clover, Heartsease
Thoughts, "You occupy my thoughts": Heartsease, Pansy
Thoughts of absent friends: Zinnia
Thoughts of heaven: Snowball
Thriftiness: Thyme

TIME: **White poplar.** The ancients traced in it a resemblance to Time, because its leaves are dark on one side and bright on the other; and for this they selected it as the emblem of day and night.

Time: Fir
Time, and philosophy: Pine

TIMIDITY: **Sensitive plant.** A flower so delicate that it shrinks from the touch, and shuns even the strong light of day, only expanding in its full beauty towards the cool of the evening. There are two or three varieties of this flower; one of which bears full, round, pink blossoms, another white, and a third yellow. Shelley has immortalised the sensitive plant in one of his most beautiful poems.

Timidity: Daphne
Timidity, "You are beautiful, but timid": Amaryllis
Token: Viburnum
Touch me not: Burdock burr
Tranquility: Rock madderwort
Tranquility, of mind: Lemon-scented geranium
Trap, "I fall into the trap laid for me": White catchfly

Travel: Mugwort
Travel, "Will you accompany me to the East?": Staphanotis
Travel, "Wilt thou go with me?": Everlasting pea
Traveler's joy: Clematis
Treachery: Sweet bay
Treason: Whortle-berry
Tree of life: Arbor vitae
Trophy, war-like: Nasturtium

Truth: **Wood hyacinth, or Blue bell.** The universal favourite of both old and young, that lights up the dark recesses of the forest, and looks as if a blue cloud had fallen from the face of heaven, and was sleeping there. It is the earliest spring flower, that bears old England's favourite colour of "true blue".

Truth: Nightshade
Truth, absolute: White chrysanthemum
Truth may be bitter: Savory

Unanimity: Phlox
Unanimous: Phlox
Uncertainty: Daffodil
Unchangeable: Globe amaranth

Unconscious beauty: **Mignonette.** A flower whose sweetness all have inhaled. It is linked to a long sentence in the Language of Flowers, and made to express, "Your qualities surpass your charms." But I have preferred making this little darling the emblem of Unconscious Beauty, as equally expressive in the sense, and more emblematical of so sweet and lowly a flower.

Understanding: Rue
Unfortunate attachment: Scabiosa
Unhappiness, "I cry for you": Elecampane
Union: Straw

United: **Lancaster rose.** Associated with history, and the union that took place between the rival houses of York and Lancaster, after the peace of England had so long been broken by their wars.

Unkindness, frozen kindness: Horehound

Unmarried, "I would be single": White rose
Unpleasant, ill nature: Crab blossom
Unselfish sharing: Tarragon
Untruth: Yellow lily
Unwelcome, "Your attentions are unwelcome": Monkshood
Usefulness: Chives, Grass
Uselessness: Meadowsweet
Utility: Grass

Valentine herb: Heartsease
Vanity, "Come down from your pedestal": Jacob's ladder
Vanity, "You are the queen of coquettes": Queen's rocket
Variety: Aster
Variety, love of: China aster
Variety, of charms: China aster
Victory: Palm, Parsley
Virgin pride: Gentian
Virtue: Rue
Virtue, domestic: Sage
Virtue, hidden: Lovage
Virtue, homely: Mint
Virtue, "Virtue makes her charming": Mountain laurel
Vision, clear: Rue
Vivacity: Houseleek
Voice, sweet: Tuberose
Voluptuousness: Tuberose
Voraciousness: Lupine

War: York and Lancaster rose, Wild tansy, Yarrow
War, "I declare war against you": Belvidere (Wild licorice),
    Wild tansy
Ward off evil: Santolina
Warmth: Cactus, Feverfew
Warmth, of feeling: Peppermint

Warmth, of heart: Red and white rose
Warmth, of sentiment: Spearmint
Weakness: Moschatel
Wealth, "I wish I were rich": King-cup
Weary, "Be not weary": Mugwort
Weather glass: Pimpernel
Wedding, wedded love: Ivy
Weep, "Why do you weep?": Chives
Welcome: Pineapple
Welcome fair stranger: Wisteria
Welcome to a stranger: Starwort
Win, resolved to win: Purple columbine
Winning grace: Cowslip
Wisdom: Cinnamon, Mint, Mulberry tree
Wish: Foxglove
Wish, "May all of your wishes come true": Camomile
Wit: Cuckoo flower
Wit, ill-timed: Sorrel
Witchcraft: Enchanter's nightshade
Witching soul of music, hers: Quaking oats
Woe: Elecampane
Woman, "The woman of the house is boss": Parsley
Woman's worth: Orange blossom
Woodland beauty: Sycamore
Worth, beyond beauty: Alyssum
Worth, "I am worthy of you": White rose
Worth, sustained by affection: Morning glory
Worthy of all praise: Fennel
Wound, "I wound to heal": Eglantine rose

Young, "You are young and beautiful": Red rosebud
Your looks freeze me: Ice plant
Youth: White lilac, Rosebud, Red and white flower, Damask rose
Youth, early: Primrose

Youth, young girl: Rosebud

Youth, "Young girl passing from childhood to youth": Primrose

Youthful gladness: Crocus

Y OUTHFUL HOPE: Snowdrop. In distinction to the Hawthorn, which is the old emblem of Hope, I have associated the Snowdrop with Youth, as it is the first flower which blows upon the edge of winter.

Youthful innocence: White lilac

Y OUTHFULNESS: Crocus. Endeared to us as one of the first flowers that breaks through the prison-house of winter, throwing a golden light upon our garden borders like the earliest sunshine of spring. It is well chosen as the emblem of Youth.

Zealousness: Elder

Zest: Lemon

APPENDICES

Ivy
"Constant friendship"

Rose   **Myrtle**
"Beauty"   *"Love"*

"To beauty, friendship, and love."

A FLORAL CALENDAR

Note: *This floral calendar is taken from* Flora's Dictionary *by E.W. Wirt, 1829.*

The Roman Catholic Monks, or the observers of Roman Catholic rules, have compiled a catalogue of Flowers, for each day in the year, and dedicated each flower to a particular Saint, on account of its flowering about the time of the Saint's festival. Such appropriations form a Floral Directory, which has been abstracted from Hone's Every Day Book, printed in London in the year 1826.

JANUARY

1. Laurustinus
2. Groundsel
3. Persian iris
4. Hazel
5. Hellebore
6. Screw moss

January the 6th, is called twelfth day, (by the French Le jour des Rois,) because it falls on the twelfth day after Christmas. There is a difference of opinion as to the origin of Twelfth Day, yet all concur in the same end; that is, to do honour to the Eastern Magi. Brand tells us, "that the practice of choosing a king on twelfth day, is similar to a custom that existed among the ancient Greeks and Romans, who on the festival days of Saturn, about this season of the year, drew lots for kingdoms, and like kings, exercised their temporary authority." Mr. Fosbroke affirms that "the king of Saturnalia was elected by beans, and from thence came our king and queen, on this day." In France the Twelfth-cake is plain, with a bean; the drawer of the slice containing the bean, is King or Queen. All drink to her or his Majesty, who reigns, and receives homage from all during the evening.

They come! they come! each blue-eyed sport,
 The Twelfth-night king, and all his court—
'Tis mirth fresh crowned with mistletoe;
 Music, with her merry fiddles,
 Joy, 'on light fantastic toe,'
Wit, with all his jests and riddles,
 Singing and dancing as they go.

7. Portuguese laurel
8. Yellow tremella
9. Laurel
10. Gorse or Furze
11. Early moss
12. Moss
13. Common yew
14. Barren strawberry
15. Ivy
16. Red dead nettle
17. Garden anemone
18. Four-toothed moss
19. White dead nettle

20. Woolly dead nettle
21. Black hellebore
22. Whitlow grass
23. Peziza
24. Stalkless moss
25. Winter hellebore

On this day, (25th Jan.) prognostications of the months were drawn for the whole year. If fair, and clear, there was to be plenty; if cloudy, or misty, much cattle would die; if rain, or snow fell, then it presaged a dearth; and if windy, there would be wars.

If Saint Paul's Day be fair and clear,
 It does betide a happy year;
But if it chance to snow or rain
 Then will be dear all kinds of grain:
If clouds, or mists, do dark the sky,
 Great store of birds and beasts shall die;
And if the winds do fly aloft,
 Then wars shall vex the kingdoms oft.

Willsford's Nature's Secrets.

St. Paul's Day, is the first festival of an Apostle, in the year. According to Dr. Foster, it is the festival of the conversion of St. Paul.

26. Coltsfoot
27. Earth moss
28. Double daisy
29. Flowering fern
30. Spleenwort
31. Hart's-tongue

FEBRUARY

1. Bay tree
2. Snowdrop
3. Water moss
4. Goldilocks
5. Primrose
6. Blue hyacinth
7. Cyclamen
8. Hair moss
9. Roman narcissus
10. Mezereon

11. Red primrose
12. Anemone
13. Polyanthus
14. Yellow crocus

The 14th of February, is the day on which those charming little missives, yclep'd Valentines, cross and intercross each other, at every street and turning. The weary, and all-for-spent twopenny postman sinks beneath a load of delicate embarrassments, not his own.

Where can the postman be, I say?
 He ought to fly-on such a day!
Of all days in the year, you know,
 It's monstrous rude to be so slow:
The fellow's so exceeding stupid—
 Hark—there he is!—oh the dear cupid.

15. Golden crocus
16. Lilac primrose
17. Scotch crocus
18. Wall speedwell
19. Field speedwell
20. Blue eyes
21. White crocus
22. Herb Margaret
23. Apricot-blossom
24. Great fern
25. Peach-blossom
26. Lesser periwinkle
27. Lungwort
28. Purple crocus
29. Purple-striped crocus

MARCH

1. Leek

Wearing the Leek, was customary in the time of Shakespeare. It is noticed in his K.H.V.
The Welshman, Fluellen, wears his leek in the battle of Agincourt.

2. Chickweed, mouse-eared
3. Golden fig
4. Chickweed, common
5. Green hellebore

6. Lent lily
7. Early daffodil
8. Great jonquil
9. Daffodil
10. Chickweed, upright
11. Cornish heath
12. Ixia
13. Heart's-ease
14. Alpine bindweed
15. Common coltsfoot
15. Lasting mercury
16. Nodding daffodil
17. Sweet violet
17. Shamrock
18. Leopard's bane, great
19. Star of Bethlehem, yellow
20. Dog's violet
21. Bulbous fumitory
22. Ficaria verva
23. Peerless daffodil
24. Golden saxifrage
25. Marigold
26. Henbane, night-shade leaved
27. Sweet jonquil
28. Leopard's bane
29. Oxlip
30. Watercress
    Daffodil, lesser
31. Benjamin-tree

APRIL

1. (All Fools Day) Mercury, French
   annual

The Romans consecrated the first day of April, to Venus, the goddess of beauty, queen of laughter, etc. It is customary on this day, to practise jocular deceptions, as various, as the fancies of the gay youngsters, who delight in playing off the humours of the day, upon all ages and ranks, that come in their way.

2. White violet
3. Evergreen alkanet
4. Crown imperial, red

5. Crown imperial, yellow
6. Hyacinth, starch
7. Wood anemone
8. Ground ivy
9. Red polyanthus
10. Pale violet
11. Dandelion
12. Saxifrage, great thick-leaved
13. Green narcissus
14. Common borage
15. Greater stitchwort
16. Yellow tulip
17. Broad-leaved arum
18. Musk narcissus
19. Garlic
20. Spring snowflake
21. Cypress narcissus
22. Wood crowfoot
23. Harebell
24. Blackthorn
25. Clarimond tulip
26. Yellow erysimon
27. Great daffodil
28. Spotted arum
29. Herb Robert
30. Cowslip

MAY

May day is chiefly spent in dancing round a tall pole, which is consecrated to the Goddess of Flowers—without the least violation to be offered to it, in the whole circle of the year.

The May-pole is up
Now give me the cup,
I'll drink to the garlands around it;
But first, unto those
Whose hands did compose
The glory of flowers that crown'd it.

Herrick

1. Tulip, Gesner
   Bachelor's button
2. Charlock
3. Poetic narcissus

4. Stock gillyflower
5. Apple tree
6. Globe flower Asiatic, bright orange
8. Lily of the valley
9. Lily of the valley
10. Peony, slender-leaved
11. Asphodel, Lancashire
12. German iris
13. Common comfrey
14. Common peony
15. Welsh poppy
16. Star of Bethlehem, great
17. Early red poppy, long rough-headed
18. Hawkweed or Mouse ear
19. Monk's hoof
20. Horse chestnut
21. Ragged robin
22. Star of Bethlehem, yellow
23. Lilac
24. Monkey poppy
25. Herb Bennet, common
26. Purple rhododendron
    Yellow azalea
27. Buttercup
    Yellow bachelor's button
28. Lurid iris
29. Blue bottle
30. Spearwort, lesser
31. Yellow Turk's-cap lily

JUNE

1. Yellow rose
2. Common scarlet pimpernel
3. Rose de meaux
4. Indian pink
5. Three-leafed China rose
6. Common ink
7. Red centaury
8. Money-wort, Herb two pence, or Creeping loose-strife
9. Barberry, Pipperidge bush of England
10. Bright yellow iris
11. Midsummer daisy

12. White dog rose
13. Garden ranunculus
14. Sweet basil
15. Sensitive plant
16. Moss province rose
17. Monkey flower, yellow
18. Horned poppy
19. LaJulienne de nuit
20. Doubtful poppy
21. Viper's bugloss
22. Canterbury bell
23. Ladies slipper
24. St. John's Wort
25. Sweet William
26. Alpine hairy blue sowthistle
27. St. John's Wort, perforated
28. Blue cornflower
29. Yellow rattle
30. Yellow cistus

JULY

1. Agrimony
2. White lily
3. Common mallow
4. Tawny day lily
5. Double yellow rose
6. Hawkweed, Purple-eyed succory
7. Nasturtium
8. Evening primrose
9. Sow-thistle, tall marsh
10. Speckled snapdragon
11. Yellow lupine
12. Great snapdragon
13. Blue lupine
14. Red lupine
15. Small cape marigold, purple and white

If it rains on St. Swithin's Day, there will be rain the next forty days afterwards.

In this month is St. Swithin's Day,
On which, if it rain, they say

Full forty days after it will
Or more, or less, some rain distill.

Poor Robin's Almanac, for the
year 1697

St. Swithin's day, if thou dost rain,
For forty days it will remain:
St. Swithin's day, if thou be fair,
For forty days 'twill rain na mair.

Hone's
E.D.B.

16. Convolvulus
17. Sweet pea
18. Autumn marigold
19. Golden hawkweed

The corolla of this flower, a rich
orange hue, contrasted with the
black hairy calyx, which gave rise to
the popular name of Grim the
collier.

20. Dragon's head, Virginian
21. Philadelphian lily
22. African lily
23. Musk flower
24. Lupine tree
25. Herb Christopher, pure white
26. Chamomile, field, or Corn fever-
    few
27. Loose strife, purple Lythrum
28. Mountain groundsel
29. Red chironia
30. White mullein
31. Yellow mullein, primrose-leafed

AUGUST

The Romish church, professing to
possess one of St. Peter's chains,
wherewith he was bound, and from
which the Angel delivered him,
indulges its votaries with a festival in
its honour, on the first day of this
month, or the Feast of St. Peter's
chains.

1. Stramony, or Thorn apple

2. Tiger lily
3. Hollyhock, Egyptian
4. Blue bells
5. Water lily, Egyptian
6. Meadow saffron
7. Common amaranth
8. Love-lies-a-bleeding
9. Yellow rag-wort
10. Balsam
11. China aster
12. Great corn sow-thistle
13. Groundsel, marsh
14. Zinnia, elegant
15. Virgin's bower, white
16. Belladonna lily
17. Snapdragon, Toad-flax
18. African marigold
19. Timothy, branched cat's tail
    grass
20. Dandelion
21. French marigold
22. Timothy, common cat's tail grass
23. Common tansy
24. Tall sunflower
25. Perennial sunflower
26. Amaryllis, banded
27. Hedge hawkweed
28. Golden-rod
29. Yellow hollyhock
30. Guernsey lily
31. Pheasant's eye

SEPTEMBER

1. Great orpine
2. Golden-rod
3. Common yellow fleabane
4. Pale pink soapwort
5. Mushroom, or Champignon
6. Dandelion
7. Golden starwort
8. Italian blue starwort

On this day (September 8th) the
Nativity of the B' V. Mary is
celebrated.

9. Golden rod, Canadian

10. Autumnal crocus
11. Variegated meadow saffron
12. Passion flower, semilunar
13. Official crocus
14. Passion flower, blue
15. Byzantine saffron
16. Sea-blue starwort
17. Narrow-leaved mallow
18. Pendulous starwort
19. Devil's bit scabious
20. Meadow saffron, common
21. Passion flower, fringed-leaved, variegated
22. Boletus tree
23. White, bushy starwort
24. Fungus
25. Great boletus
26. Great golden rod
27. White starwort, white and small-leaved
28. Golden rod, evergreen
29. Michaelmas daisy
30. Golden amaryllis

OCTOBER

1. Lowly amaryllis
2. Soapwort
3. Downy helenium
4. Southernwood, dwarf
5. Star-like chamomile
6. Feverfew, creeping
7. Indian chrysanthemum
8. Sweet maudlin
9. Milky mushroom
10. Cape waved-leaved aletris
11. Common holly
12. Wavy fleabane
13. Yellow helenium, smooth
14. Indian fleabane
15. Sweet sultan, purple
16. Yarrow
17. Dwarf sunflower
18. Mushroom
19. Tick-seed, perennial
20. Sweet Sultan, yellow
21. Silphium, hairy-stalked

22. Silphium, rough, three-leaved
23. Starwort, slender-stalked
24. Starwort, Carolina
25. Starwort, fleabane
26. Golden rod, late flowering
27. Starwort, floribund
28. Chrysanthemum, late flowering, creeping
    Starwort, scattered
29. Narcissus, green autumnal
30. Mixen mushroom
31. Tick-seed, fennel-leaved

The 31st October is all Hallow E'en, or the vigil of All Saint's Day, in which young people try their fortune, by drawing cabbages from the ground, blindfolded. Or, burning nuts in the fire, etc.

The cabbage, or kale, being large or small, straight or crooked, is deemed prophetic of the size and form of the grand object of their spells. If any earth adhere to the root, that is tocher, or fortune; the taste of the heart of the stem, is indicative of the natural temper and disposition. Lastly, the stems are placed over the door, and the christian name of the person who first enters through the door, will be the name sought for. If more than one be so affixed, it will be decided according to the priority of placing the runts or stalks.

The nuts are named, and accordingly as they burn quietly together, or start from beside each other, the course, and issue of their love will be.

These glowing nuts are emblems true
 Of what in human life we view;
The ill-matched couple fret and fume,
 And thus, in strife themselves consume;
Or, from each other wildly start,
 And with a noise for ever part.

But see, the happy, happy pair,
  Of genuine love and truth sincere;
With mutual fondness, while they burn,
  Still to each other kindly turn,
And as the vital sparks decay,
  Together gently sink away:
Till life's fierce ordeal being past,
  Their mingled ashes rest at last.

Charles Graydon, Esq., from his
  collection of poems. Dublin,
  1801

NOVEMBER

1. Laurustinus
2. Winter cherry
3. Primrose
4. Strawberry tree
5. Common winter cherry, orange
   coloured fruit
6. Common yew tree
7. Large furcroa
8. Cape aletris
9. Aletris, glaucous-leafed
10. Scotch fir
11. Weymouth pine
12. Aloe, great orange flowering
13. Bay
14. Laurel, Portugal
15. Coltsfoot, sweet-scented
16. African bow-string hemp
17. Thorn apple tree
18. Passion flower, notched-leafed
19. Passion flower, apple fruited
20. Red stapelia
21. Wood sorrel
22. Wood sorrel, tube-flowered

St. Cecilia, a Sicilian Martyr. She
is the titular Saint and Patroness of
Music, particularly of Sacred Music.
She is supposed to be the inventress
of the organ; and to have drawn
down an Angel from Heaven by the
music of her voice.

At last divine Cecilia came,
  Inventress of the vocal frame;
The sweet enthusiast, from her sacred store,

Enlarg'd the former narrow bounds,
  And added length, to solemn sounds,
With Nature's Mother-wit, and arts
unknown before.
Let old Timotheus yield the prize,
  Or both divide the crown:
He rais'd a mortal to the skies:
  She brought an Angel down.

Dryden

23. Sorrel, convex
24. Starry stapelia
25. Sweet butterbur
26. Sorrel, Linnear
27. Sorrel, lupine-leaved
28. Stapelia, variegated
29. Sphenogyne
30. Sorrel, three-coloured

November 30th is St. Andrew's
Day, Patron saint of Scotland, one of
the Apostles. A Martyr. The form of
the cross of St. Andrew, is believed
to be that of the letter X, styled a
cross Decussate. The Muscovites, say
he preached among them, and claim
him as the titular saint of their
empire.

DECEMBER

1. Stapelia, dark
2. Lemon geodurum
3. Indian tree
4. Gooseberry, Barbadoes
5. Hibiscus, long stalked
6. Heath, nest-flowered
7. Achania, hairy
8. Arbor vitae, American
9. Corsican spruce
10. Portugal cypress
11. Aleppo pine
12. Heath, crowded
13. Arbor vitae, African
14. Swamp pine
15. Pitch pine
16. Arbor vitae, Chinese
17. White cedar

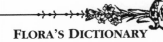

18. New Holland cypress
19. Heath, two-coloured
20. Stone pine
21. Sparrow-wort
22. Pellucid heath
23. Cedar of Lebanon
24. Frankincense pine
25. Holly

Some say, that ever 'against that season comes
 Wherein our Saviour's birth is celebrated,
This bird of dawning singeth all night long.
 And then, they say, no spirit stirs abroad;
The nights are wholesome;
 then no planet strikes;
No fairy takes, nor witch
 hath power to charm—
So hallow'd, and so gracious is the time.

    Shakespeare, Hamlet

Christmas, the joyous period of the year!
Now with bright Holly all the temples strow,
With Laurel, green and sacred Mistletoe.
    Gay

With Holly and Ivy,
 So green and so gay,
We deck up our houses
 As fresh as the day,
With bays, and rosemary,
 And laurel complete;

And ever one now
 Is a king in conceit.

    From Poor Robin's Almanac, for
      1695

26. Purple heath
27. Flame heath
28. Heath, bloody-flowered
29. Heath
30. Ponthieva, glandular
31. Winter jasmine

If New Year's eve night-winds blow South,
 It betokens warmth and growth;
If West, much milk, and fish in the sea;
 If North, much cold, and storms there will
 be;
If East, the trees will bear much fruit;
 If North-east, flee it man and brute.
And the next to this is New-Year's day,
 Whereon to every frende,
They costly presents in do bring,
 And New-Year's gifts do sende.
These gifts the husband gives his wife,
 And father eke the childe,
And master on his men bestowes
 The like, with favour milde.

    From the Latin of Thomas
      Naogeorgus, 1553, translated by
      Barnarbe Googe

FANFARE OF COLOR EMBLEMS

Plant meanings can be derived from flower color if no other basis is evident. The following is translated from Emma Faucon's Le Langage des Fleurs.

Amaranth {reddish-purple} : constancy, immortal
Black: sadness, death, mourning
Blue: pure love, economy, wisdom, respect, piety
Dark brown: deep grief
Green: hope, maritime, childhood
Gray: moderate grief, melancholy
Lavender: pure love
Orange: love of glory
Purple: sovereignty, power, pride, ambition
Red: timidity, love, passion
Rose: beauty, love, friendliness, youth
White: innocence, purity, cleanness, timidity, good faith

FLOWER
BY THE HOUR

A Victorian garden novelty was a garden bed arranged in a pattern that could tell time by the hour that the flowers opened and closed their blossoms. The state of perfection of a flower was thought to be the time of flowering, and was called "the joy of plants." It was keenly observed that flowers opened and closed at different times. This fascination led to the composition of a garden bed, perhaps even in the shape of a clock, which could tell the time with the blossoms—a dial of flowers.

Floral dictionaries suggested flowers which could be grown in this floral clock. Particular attention was paid to the conditions needed for flowering, as well as the exact hour that the flowers opened and closed. A flower was needed to open or close at all hours of the day and night.

> Some plants habitually open and close their flowers by turns; others are governed in these respects by the weather; others again, by the length or shortness of the day; while some open and shut at certain hours, and thus furnish materials for composing the Dial of Flowers.
>
> *The Floral Offering,* 1868

To tell time by the flowers was a popular Victorian pursuit. The ladies were encouraged to observe nature and choose from the many flowers available to form their floral clock. Suggested inclusions were listed.

> These properties of flowers, and the opening and shutting of many at particular times of the day, led to the idea of planting them in such a manner as to indicate the succession of the hours, and to make them supply the place of a watch or clock. Those who are disposed to try the experiment may easily compose such a dial by consulting the following table, comprehending the hours between three in the morning and eight in the evening.
>
> *The Floral Offering,* 1868

The author acknowledged that the accuracy of this floral clock was not ensured due to the nature of plants and unforeseen conditions in the weather. The pursuit of creating a parterre as a Dial of Flowers, however, was still enthusiastically encouraged.

THE DIAL OF FLOWERS

From *Flora's Lexicon*, 1868.

Names of Plants	Hours of opening	Hours of shutting
Yellow goat's beard *Tragopogon luteum*	3	
Common base hawkweed *Crepis tectorum*	4	
Field sowthistle *Sonchus agrestis*	5	
Dandelion *Leontodon taraxacum*	5	
Alpine base hawkweed *Crepis alpina*	5	
Naked-stalked poppy *Papaver nudicaule*	5	
Orange day-lily *Hemerocallis fulva*	5	
Red hawkweed *Hieracium rubrum*	5–6	
Meadow goshmore *Hypochaeris pratensis*	6	
Red base hawkweed *Crepis rubra*	6½	
White water lily *Nymphoea alba*	7	
White spiderwort *Anthericum album*	7	
Tongue-leafed mesembryanthemum *Mesembryanthemum linguiforme*	7–8	
Bearded mesembryanthemum *M. barbatum*	8	
Dandelion *Leontodon taraxacum*	...	8–9
Yellow goat's beard *Tragopogon luteum*	...	9
Field marigold *Calendula arvensis*	9	
Single-flowered hawkweed *Hieracium pilosella*	9	

Names of Plants	Hours of opening	Hours of shutting
Red sandwort *Arenaria rubra*	10	
Ice plant *Mesembryanthemum crystallinum*	10	
Common base hawkweed *Crepis tectorum*	...	11
Alpine base hawkweed *Crepis alpina*	...	11
Field sowthistle *Sonchus agrestis*	...	12
Red pink *Dianthus prolifer*	...	1
Red base hawkweed *Crepis rubra*	...	1
Bearded mesembryanthemum *M. barbatum*	...	2
Single-flowered hawkweed *Hieracium pilosella*	...	2
Red sandwort *Arenaria rubra*	...	3
Field marigold *Calendula arvensis*	...	3
Tongue-leafed mesembryanthemum *M. linguiforme*	...	3
Red hawkweed *Hieracium rubrum*	...	4
Ice plant *Mesembryanthemum crystallinum*	...	4
White spiderwort *Anthericum album*	...	4
Meadow goshmore *Hypochoeris pratensis*	...	5
White water lily *Nymphoea alba*	...	6
Naked-stalked poppy *Papaver nudicaule*	...	7
Orange day-lily *Hemerocallis fulva*	...	8

REFERENCES AND FURTHER READING

ANTIQUE FLORAL DICTIONARIES

Illustrations and text for this book were taken from the following antiquarian sources:

Adams, H. G. *The Language and Poetry of Flowers.* Philadelphia: J.B. Lippincott & Co., 1864; 1866.

Adams, John S., ed. *Flora's Album: The language of flowers.* Boston: Elias Howe, 1847.

Anonymous. *The Diamond Florist.* London: Ackermann & Co., 1836.

Anonymous. *The Language and Poetry of Flowers.* London: George Routledge and Sons, n.d.

Anonymous. *The Language of Flowers,* second edition. Philadelphia: Carey, Lea and Blanchard, 1835.

Anonymous. *The Language of Flowers and Floral Poesy: A book for all seasons.* New York: John W. Lovell, n.d.

Anonymous. *The Language of Flowers: Flora's album.* New York: Leavitt & Allen, 1853.

Anonymous. *The Language of Flowers, including Floral Poetry.* London: Frederick Warne And Co., 1884.

Anonymous. *The Language of Flowers.* London: James Williams, 1844.

Anonymous. *Pansies For Thoughts.* New York: E. P. Dutton & Co., n.d.

Anonymous. *The Sentiment of Flowers, or Language of Flora.* Illustrated by James Andrews. Philadelphia: Lea and Blanchard, 1840.

Bourne, H. *The Florist's Manual.* Boston: Munroe and Francis, 1833.

Burke, L., ed. *The Illustrated Language and Poetry of Flowers.* London: George Routledge and Sons, n.d.

Dinnies, Anna Peyre. *The Floral Year.* Boston: Benjamin B. Mussey, 1847.

Dugdale, Rose Sydenham. *A Wreath of Flower Legends.* Great Britain: The Weather Oak Press Limited, 1850.

Dumont, Henrietta. *The Floral Offering: The language and poetry of flowers*. Philadelphia: Theodore Bliss and Company, 1868.

Edgarton, S. C. *The Flower Vase: The language of flowers*. Lowell: Merrill and Heywood, 1844; 1847; 1848.

Faucon, Emma. *Le Langage des Fleurs*. Paris: Lefevre, n.d.

Greenwood, Laura, ed. *The Rural Wreath, or Life Among the Flowers*. Boston: Dayton and Wentworth, 1855; 1856.

Hale, Sarah Josepha. *Flora's Interpreter: The American book of flowers and sentiments*. Boston: Thomas H. Webb and Company, 1833; 1849; 1856.

Hooper, Lucy, ed. *The Lady's Book of Flowers and Poetry: A complete floral dictionary*. New York: J. C. Riker, 1843; 1864.

L.H. *A Floral Souvenir. A perennial gift with a complete floral dictionary*. Chambersburg, PA: Shryock, Reed and Company, 1841.

Osgood, Frances S., ed. *The Poetry of Flowers, and Flowers of Poetry*. New York: J. C. Riker, 1852.

Sutton, Adah Louise. *When Roses Bloom*. New York: The Saalfield Publishing Co., n.d.

Tyas, Robert. *The Language of Flowers, or Floral Emblems of Thoughts, Feelings, and Sentiments*. London: George Routledge and Sons, 1869.

Waterman, Catherine H. *Flora's Lexicon: An interpretation of the language and sentiment of flowers*. Philadelphia: Herman Hooker, 1839.

Wirt, E. W. *Flora's Dictionary*. Baltimore: Fielding Lucas Jr., 1829; 1833.

FURTHER READING

Addison, Josephine. *The Illustrated Plant Lore*. London: Sedgwick and Jackson Limited, 1985.

Angel, Marie. *A Floral Calendar and Other Flower Lore*. London: Pelham Books Ltd, 1985.

Burke, Mrs. L. *The Language of Flowers*. Los Angeles: Price Stern Sloan Publishers, Inc., 1965. (Published in 1963 by Hugh Evelyn Limited, London.)

Campbell, Mary Mason; Greeley, Deborah Webster; Lord, Priscilla Sawyer; Morss, Elisabeth W. *A Basket of Herbs: A book of American sentiments*. Illustrations by Tasha Tudor. Brattleboro, Vermont: The Stephen Greene Press, 1983.

Crowell, Robert L. *The Lore and Legends of Flowers*. New York: Thomas Y. Crowell, 1982.

Earle, Alice Morse. *Old Time Gardens*. New York: The Macmillan Company, 1901.

Ely, Helena Rutherfurd. *A Woman's Hardy Garden*. New York: Grosset and Dunlap, 1903.

F.W.H. *The Language of Flowers*. London: Waterlows, 1968. (Reprint of an anniversary gift handwritten "To Mother, from Father" in 1913.)

Greenaway, Kate. *Language of Flowers*. New York: Gramercy Publishing Company, 1978. (Reprint of the 1884 edition published by G. Routledge, London.)

Grieve, Mrs. M. *A Modern Herbal*. (Two volumes.) New York: Dover Publications, 1971. (Republication of the work originally published by Harcourt, Brace and Company, 1931.)

Laufer, Geraldine Adamich. *Tussie-Mussies: The Victorian art of expressing yourself in the language of flowers*. New York: Workman Publishing Company, Inc., 1993.

Marsh, Jean. *The Illuminated Language of Flowers*. New York: Holt, Rinehart, and Winston, 1978.

Martin, Laura C. *Garden Flower Folklore*. Chester, Connecticut: Globe Pequot Press, 1987.

Moretz, James. *Posy Bouquet Holders*. Chicago: Flowerian Publishers, 1984.

Peroni, Laura. *The Language of Flowers*. New York: Crown Publishers, 1884.

Pickles, Sheila, ed. *The Language of Flowers*. New York: Harmony Books, 1990.

Pickles, Sheila, ed. *A Victorian Posy*. London: Pavilion Books, 1987.

Powell, Claire. *The Meaning of Flowers: A garland of plant lore and symbolism from popular custom and literature*. London: Jupiter Books, 1977.

Roberts, Victoria Stanhope. *A Pleasure of Flowers*. San Francisco: Strawberry Hill Press, 1977.

Schwartz, Jeri. *Tussie Mussies: Victorian posy holders*. Tarrytown, New York: Schwartz, 1987.

Stuart, Malcolm. *Herbs and Herbalism*. London: Van Nostrand Reinhold, 1979.

Todd, Pamela. *Forget-Me-Not: A floral treasury. Sentiments and plant lore from the language of flowers*. Boston: Little, Brown, 1993.

Westland, Pamela. *Victorian Nosegays*. New York: Crescent Books, 1991.

Wilson, Helen Van Pelt. *Geraniums, Pelargoniums*. New York: M. Barrows, 1946.

SOURCES

SOURCES FOR ANTIQUARIAN BOTANICAL BOOKS

Sometimes a floral dictionary from the last century can be found in a stack of dusty books at a flea market or old book store and can be purchased by the lucky buyer for a few dollars. More often, however, they must be searched for in bookstores that specialize in antique botanicals. Since many of these treasured books have plates that have been hand-colored, they command a high price. Depending on whether the book is complete (that is, has had no plates removed), the condition of the cover and binding, and the age, the price can range from hundreds to thousands of dollars each. According to Elizabeth Woodburn Books, a complete copy of Mrs. Wirt's floral dictionary with 58 hand-colored plates sold for over three thousand dollars a few years ago.

The following are sources for additional books on the language of flowers or antiquarian botanical books by mail-order. Many offer specialized searches for any book that is requested.

The American Botanist Booksellers
PO Box 532
Chillicothe, IL 61523
309-274-5254

Catalog: Free. Specializing in agriculture, horticulture, olericulture, and their history.

Elizabeth Woodburn Books
Booknoll Farm
PO Box 398
Hopewell, NJ 08525
609-466-0522

A member of the Antiquarian Booksellers Association of America. Old and new books on horticulture, landscape gardening, herbs, and early farming.

Pomona Book Exchange
PO Box 111
Rockton, Ontario
L0R 1X0 CANADA
519-621-8897

Catalog: Free. Dealing in the literature of pomology and general horticulture with books that are out-of-print, new, and rare. You may visit and browse through the bookroom. Phone ahead for an appointment.

Second Life Books
PO Box 242, 55 Quarry Road
Lanesborough, MA 01237
413-447-8010
FAX 413-499-1540

Catalog: Free. Offering a collection of rare books in agriculture, horticulture, and the rural arts from the sixteenth to the twentieth centuries. All books are available for browsing throughout the year; call or write for directions.

Wood Violet Books
3814 Sunhill Drive
Madison, WI 53704
608-837-7207

Catalog: $2.00. Wood Violet Books is a bookstore that specializes in herb and garden books with a selection of herb craft books and garden cookbooks. Special orders are always welcome.

SOURCES FOR TUSSIE-MUSSIES, POSY PINS, AND FLORIGRAPHY

The Rosemary House
120 S. Market St.
Mechanicsburg PA 17055
717-697-5111

Catalog $2.00. Herbal wedding supplies, tussie-mussies, hand-held posy holders.

Betsy Williams
The Proper Season
155 Chestnut St.
Andover MA 01810

Catalog $1.00. Wedding and friendship herbs and wreaths, herbal wedding booklet.

Greenfield Herb Garden
1135 Woodbine
Oak Park IL 60302
219-768-7110

Catalog $1.50. Tussie-mussie Bouquet Doilies, Everlastings.

Village Herb Shop Catalog & Herbal Handbook
152 S. Main St.
Chagrin Falls OH 44022
216-247-5039

Catalog $4.00. Tussie-mussie recipe, tussie-mussie kits (fresh and dried), tussie-mussies in several styles. Large selection of posy pins, florigraphy books, hand-held posy holders.

Rasland Farm
NC 82 at US 13
Godwin NC 28344

Catalog $2.50. Wedding and bridal gifts, tussie-mussies and bouquets, dried bunches of hanging herbs.

Elizabeth Woodburn
Antiquarian book seller

Thyme - disinfectant
Mint - step on it

The Language of Flowers
Geraldine Adanich
Every plant by God for use Toufen
Floral dictionary - small

Aromatherapy to sleep   Forbes 2-27-06
- Zanzibar Mist: oils of lemon grass, ylang ylang (flower of tropical tree) coconut
- Insomnia Relief Scent Inhaler
lavender, rosemary, chamomile & vetiver (grass root)

ABOUT THE AUTHOR

Twentieth-century herbarist Kathleen Gips has been growing, using, studying, and writing about herbs for nearly 20 years. Her main area of research has been the tussie-mussie, or herbal nosegay, and the language of herbs and flowers. She owns an extensive collection of antique floral dictionaries and posy holders that compliment that research. Her first book, *The Language of Flowers: A Book of Victorian Floral Sentiments,* was published in 1987, and an expanded edition was introduced in 1990. This work documents the use of floral symbolism in the 1800s and has been welcomed throughout the country as a much-needed reference on the subject. *Flora's Dictionary: The Victorian Language of Herbs and Flowers* is the most recent expansion of that research.

Ms. Gips has published numerous articles on this and other herbal subjects and has served as editor of two publications of The Herb Society of America. She lectures frequently at garden clubs, herb societies, and symposia, and has presented classes at the Greater Cleveland Botanical Garden, of which she is a member. She is also a member of the The Herb Society of America, the American Horticultural Society, the Heritage Rose Foundation, and the International Herb Association.

In addition to writing, lecturing, and teaching about herbs and floral language, Ms. Gips has since 1979 successfully operated a small herb products business called Pine Creek Herbs in her home town of Chagrin Falls, Ohio. In 1989 she opened a retail shop and mail-order business there called the Village Herb Shop Catalog. She leads an active and herb-centered life in Chagrin Falls with her husband, Jack.

ORDER FORM
(for copying)

Fax orders: (216) 247-1492

Phone orders: call toll free (800) 836-9120
(orders only, please). Give name, shipping address,
and VISA/MasterCard number with expiration date.

Postal orders: Send a copy of this form to
TM Publications, 152 S. Main St.,
Chagrin Falls OH 44022 USA

Customer service telephone: (216) 247-5039

Please send ***Flora's Dictionary: The Victorian
Language of Herbs and Flowers***
_____ copies @ $16.95 $_____

Please send ***The Village Herb Shop Catalog
and Herbal Handbook***
_____ copies @ $4.00 $_____

Add 7% sales tax for books
shipped to Ohio addresses $_____

Shipping: $_____
Surface, book rate: (allow 3-4 weeks for delivery)
$2.00 first book, $.75 each additional book
Air mail: $3.50 per book

Total order $_____

Company: _____

Name: _____

Address: _____

City: _____ **State:** ____ **Zip:** _____

Telephone: (_____) _____

❑ Check or money order enclosed
❑ VISA ❑ MasterCard

Card number: _____

Name on card: _____

Expiration: _____